Praise for
DeVon Franklin

"DeVon Franklin is a bona fide dynamo . . . a different kind of spiritual leader for our times."

—Oprah Winfrey

"In the twenty years I've known DeVon, he's lived his life the same way he makes his movies: with commitment, humility, and a work ethic that demands respect."

—Will Smith

"DeVon's message is for anyone seeking to strike that quintessential balance between faith and function. Hollywood, like life, is a walk of faith."

—T.D. Jakes

THE TRUTH ABOUT MEN

What Men and Women Need to Know

DeVON FRANKLIN

ATRIA PAPERBACK

NEW YORK   LONDON   TORONTO   SYDNEY   NEW DELHI

ATRIA
PAPERBACK

An Imprint of Simon & Schuster, Inc.
1230 Avenue of the Americas
New York, NY 10020

First Atria Paperback edition February 2020

ATRIA PAPERBACK and colophon are trademarks of Simon & Schuster, Inc.

For information about special discounts for bulk purchases, please contact Simon & Schuster Special Sales at 1-866-506-1949 or business@simonandschuster.com.

The Simon & Schuster Speakers Bureau can bring authors to your live event. For more information or to book an event, contact the Simon & Schuster Speakers Bureau at 1-866-248-3049 or visit our website at www.simonspeakers.com.

Manufactured in the United States of America

1 3 5 7 9 10 8 6 4 2

Library of Congress Control Number: 2018033175

ISBN 978-1-9821-0127-5
ISBN 978-1-9821-0128-2 (pbk)
ISBN 978-1-9821-0129-9 (ebook)

To Love

Contents

The Truth
About Men

Are Men Really Dogs?

Why must I feel that? Why must I chase the cat?
Nothing but the dog in me!
—GEORGE CLINTON, "ATOMIC DOG"

I almost didn't write this book. While I was on the promotional tour for my previous book, *The Hollywood Commandments*, I decided I was going to take a break from writing for a while. I love writing, but I thought it was time to give it a breather and focus on other aspects of my career.

But then one conversation changed everything. Maria Shriver was interviewing me for her Facebook show *Architects of Change* as part of my tour. After the cameras stopped rolling, I was talking with her and her staff. This was in the fall of 2017, right around the time the news of Harvey Weinstein's sexual assault scandal broke. Inevitably, we started talking about this and I said to her, off the cuff, "I've always wanted to write a book called *Are Men Really Dogs?*"

I went on to tell her why I believe men behave badly—why so many men seem to chase after money and power and sex, no matter the cost—and started laying out solutions for how men can take responsibility for and correct the problem. I also started talking about what women need to know about what's really going on inside a man. Maria stopped me and said, "You must write this book right now!"

I told her no. I had just released a book and I was going to take a break. She persisted, and I said, "Okay, I'll think about it." That was just my way of placating her, because I had no intention of taking on a topic as big and as potentially divisive as this one.

But I couldn't stop thinking about it. And the more I thought about it, the more convinced I became that I wanted nothing to do with this idea. It's dangerous to write a book about what men need to do better. First of all, most men don't like looking in the mirror (I know I don't), and this would be asking them to do just that. But not only that: taking on a topic like this would require me to examine my own manhood and discuss it honestly and transparently. I spend a lot of time talking to other people about having faith and facing their fears. Writing a book like this would challenge me to do the exact same thing; it's not enough to tell others what to do if I don't do it myself. I have to "walk it like I talk it," and I couldn't imagine too many things that would be more frightening. However, I felt compelled that this is what I must do, so I decided to face my fears and speak my truth.

WHAT'S REALLY GOING ON?

In his song "Against All Odds," the late Tupac Shakur, arguably one of the greatest rappers in history, spoke a famous line: "This be the realest sh*t I ever wrote." That line resonates with me because it expresses exactly how I feel about this book. Of all the books I've written, this is the most timely, relevant, urgent, and personal.

I'm a Hollywood producer and a preacher, and people often ask me why men act the way they do. Those questions didn't start with the tsunami of sexual harassment allegations we started hearing about in the news in late 2017; however, they have intensified since the news about Harvey Weinstein sparked and encouraged legions of women to come forward about the way men have mistreated and/or abused them. I realized that in order to really uncover the issue and the root of men's behavior, I needed to start by looking at my own life and family history.

I was raised in Oakland, California, by my mother, my grandmother, and my grandmother's seven sisters—my great-aunts. Because I was raised predominantly by women and spent so much time with them, I saw firsthand the pain that the many men in their lives caused them, primarily due to infidelity. As a young kid I was so perplexed by this that I asked them, "Can a man be faithful?" They responded unanimously, saying, "No. Ninety-nine percent of all men cheat."

What?! No way, I thought. I was devastated. It sounded like they were citing a fundamental law of the universe.

Growing up, I heard (and still hear even now) the following refrain:

All men cheat.
Men can't be faithful.
Men can't keep it in their pants.
Men love power.
Men are greedy.
Men are dogs.

I became fascinated by the question "Are men really dogs?"

It was a personal question for me, because my father, Donald Ray Franklin, wasn't around much when my brothers and I were growing up. He struggled with alcoholism our entire lives, and when he was just thirty-six (I was nine at the time) he died of a heart attack. Years after his passing, when I was a teenager, I was at one of my cousin's houses and found a photo of my dad sitting on a bed next to a female family member. My mother was sitting on the same bed, but on the opposite side. Strangely, my dad and this family member were smiling, while my mother looked distraught. I asked someone else in the family, "Do you know why my mother looks so upset in this photo?"

This person told me a truth that rocked me to my core, one I've never expressed publicly until now: My dad had cheated on my mom with another woman in my family.

Damn.

How could this have happened? My own father cheated on my mother with another woman—in my family?! I drew a quick conclusion: *Maybe men really are dogs.*

And if my father was one, I realized, that must make me one too.

This revelation threw me into disbelief. I decided I didn't want to become part of the ninety-nine percent. I didn't want to become a dog or act like one.

This revelation also sparked my quiet obsession with discovering the answer to two questions: *What is going on inside men?* and *Is something wrong with us?*

As I thought about these questions, I found the easiest response was to take the self-righteous path and assume I would never be like that. Yet as I grew into adulthood, I noticed that deep inside me was a growing and seemingly insatiable appetite for sex, women, money, power, and success. Appalled, I found myself consistently suppressing these desires—trying to live as if they didn't exist. But again and again, I found the power of these urges to be overwhelming at times.

Recently, society got a reminder of that power in the avalanche of sexual assault allegations leveled against some of the most prominent, powerful men in the world. As the stories started erupting out of Hollywood (from Harvey Weinstein to Kevin Spacey), politics (from John Conyers to Al Franken), sports (from Larry Nassar to Jerry Richardson), and other dominant industries, I began to ask myself—as did many others— "How could so many well-known, highly accomplished men get to a place where they allowed their urges to control them, consume them, and eventually destroy their lives?" How could countless men throughout history until this very day have such a difficult time remaining faithful? It seemed beyond explanation.

These questions are not meant to be shots fired, point fingers, or be expressions of self-righteous indignation. They are part of an honest, anguished search for answers about what really haunts men no matter our age, race, or position in society. I ask questions like this about my own life:

- How could my dad cheat on my mom with another woman?
- How could I have impure thoughts and urges that don't seem to go away with prayer or fasting?
- Why do I sometimes think about other women, even though I love my wife?

It's important that I make something clear: *There's a difference between being a harasser and having difficulty controlling urges that could lead to infidelity.* I'm not trying to put these things in the same category or paint them with the same broad brush, because the physical assault and violation of women is indefensible. Most men have issues managing their urges, but most of those same men would never think of sexually or physically assaulting a woman.

I don't smoke weed and I'm a not proponent of it; however, I'm told there are many different materials that can be derived from the *Cannabis sativa* plant. Hemp stalk is a strong natural fiber, with no hallucinogenic properties, that can be used to make clothing and other materials, while marijuana comes from the flowers of the plant. Hemp seeds are high in protein, amino acids, and essential fatty acids and vitamins, and are sometimes considered a superfood. They all have different purposes and properties, but hemp stalk, hemp seeds, and marijuana all come from the same plant.

The same goes for men's issues—they can take many forms, yet I believe they all stem from the same root.

THE LUST PROBLEM

The Me Too Movement actually predates the hashtag that gained popularity in late 2017. It was started in 2006 by Tarana Burke, who founded the movement "to help survivors of sexual violence, particularly young women of color from low wealth communities, find pathways to healing. . . . the me too. movement was ultimately created to ensure survivors know they're not alone in their journey." Then it was adopted widely in the wake of the sexual harassment scandals, and it became a way for women who have been victims of sexual harassment and assault to speak out about their abuse—many for the first time. In December 2017, the #MeToo "Silence Breakers" were named *Time*'s Person of the Year. According to #MeToo, 17,700,000 women have reported a sexual assault since 1998—and that's just those who have *reported* it.

Time's Up is a crusade against sexual harassment that started in January 2018 by a group of three hundred women in Hollywood.

It has a similar vision for women's empowerment as #MeToo, but it functions as a next step in the movement with solution-based, action-oriented advocacy aimed at creating significant change, safety, and equity in the workplace.

In the wake of the powerful and timely #MeToo and #TimesUp movements that started because of the wave of sexual assault allegations, I began to look for the root cause of sexual harassment and assault. Could the same fidelity and greed issues most men struggle with come from the same root?

As I've delved deeper into my own life and also analyzed what's really going on with other men, I've realized there is an issue that no one's talking about: *Men have a lust problem.*

This is the secret that men carry.

While much of my focus throughout this book will be on sexual desire, lust is more than just a hunger for sex. Here is my definition:

Lust is an overwhelming selfish impulse for sexual, financial, professional, or personal fulfillment by any means necessary, even if those means are personally, professionally, or spiritually detrimental.

I call this lust *the Dog.*

Every man has lust, aka the Dog, within him, and when we allow that lust to go untrained, unmanaged, and unmastered, it can cause men to behave just like an untrained dog. When fed, this Dog can become powerful enough to destroy every good thing men have planned for their lives.

Our society is in a state of emergency because of unmanaged lust running rampant in men. As a result, men are causing untold damage to women, themselves, their families, and our communities.

DOG TRAINING

The most important benefit of training your dog is safety: your safety, the safety of others, and his own safety . . . a trained dog is a free dog.

—JACK & WENDY VOLHARD, *DOG TRAINING FOR DUMMIES*

Have you ever owned a dog that wasn't trained? What happened when you left it alone all day? Do you remember coming home to find torn-up couch cushions, shredded shoes, and everything in chaos? Now imagine that house is your life. If men don't train the Dog within, what kind of destruction will continue to happen to their relationships, careers, and reputations?

The Dog hungers for vice, women, money, power, and possessions. It covets success. It looks for any kind of instant gratification. The Dog hates monogamy, restraint, and patience. But what makes the Dog really dangerous is that it is never satisfied. You can feed it vice until you think it's full, but its appetite only grows. The Dog wants what it wants when it wants it.

None of this is meant to excuse infidelity or bad behavior. Recognizing that the Dog exists is not the same as approving of it. Instead, it's recognition of a stark reality:

If the man doesn't master the Dog, the Dog will master the man.

When men cheat on their girlfriends or wives, the Dog is in control. When men lie, cheat, or steal to get ahead in life, the Dog is in control. Men all around the world, from all eras and all stations in life, from priests and ministers to poets and presidents, have struggled with the Dog. Even in the Scriptures, we find accounts of men, from King David to Samson to the apostle Paul, who confessed to having trouble dealing with the Dog within them. From Julius Caesar to Caligula, history is filled with stories of men who had trouble with the Dog. And while it isn't exactly clear when society started referring to men as "dogs," in many traditions (including Islam and Rabbinic Judaism) dogs have historically been associated with violence, uncleanliness, and sexual promiscuity. In an article on when Muslims began to have a negative perception of dogs for *Quartz India*, Alan Mikhail writes, "This idea taps into a long tradition that considers even the mere sight of a dog during prayer to have the power to nullify a pious Muslim's supplications."

Every man has lust in him. Every man has the Dog in him. That's the bad news.

The good news? Every man also has love in him.

I call this love *the Master.* Every dog has a master. Every man has a Dog and every man has a Master within. The cure for the problem of the Dog is *Mastery.*

The Master represents the love in a man—the love of self, love of family, love of the woman in his life, the love of community. There's enough love in a man to counteract the lust in a man. I believe every man truly wants to love and be loved. However, as men we aren't taught how to love. Most men stumble in this area of learning what it means to love, especially self-love. This is why Mastery must be practiced, because the more men practice love and being loving, the stronger the Master will become. When the Master is in control, the Dog must obey. Mastering love is the key to everything, because the Dog cannot be eliminated—it can only be mastered. *Mastery*, as I define it, is the practice of learning to love. Without Mastery, the Dog leads men to act against marriage vows and damage their integrity, and it even changes the fiber of a man's character. In order for men to be truly successful, there must be recognition that the Dog has the power to destroy and a choice must be made to discipline it. Love is indeed the most powerful force in the universe and that's why the love—aka the Master—in men must be empowered, developed, and unleashed.

The Master knows how to honor himself and the women in his life. He's respectful and consistent. He's a warrior for peace and well-being. He craves responsibility and accepts accountability. He's a builder who creates a happy home and a strong family because they are the most important things in his life. He's at his best, fully expressing his potential. He's thoughtful and compassionate. He's sexy because he can handle commitment. He's a *man*, not a boy in a man's body. Most of all, a Master bows to The Master. He understands that the true power to tame the Dog comes from above.

Mastering the Dog is dangerous work. Why? Because it requires a combination of transparency and discipline that men rarely employ. How do men master the Dog? By committing to training it.

Training is everything, and it's the key to success. Noted dog trainers Jack and Wendy Volhard say this about training: "After all, a well-trained dog is a happy dog, and happy dogs have happy owners. However, you can't expect a dog to do what you want him to do (or don't want to do) unless you show him what your expectations are. And your dog won't learn properly or be willing to heed your commands unless you use effective training methods."

THE TRUTH ABOUT MEN: WHAT MEN AND WOMEN NEED TO KNOW

It's time for us as men to do our work, because we are the problem. For too long we have placed the responsibility of our poor behavior at the feet of women. It's time for men to "man up" and allow the buck to stop with us.

However, we generally don't like to do our work. We're stubborn and resistant to looking in the mirror and acknowledging that we have to change.

A 2015 clip of DJ Khaled's appearance on Power 105's *The Breakfast Club* went viral because of his views on gender roles. He said, "You gotta understand, I'm the don. I'm the king . . . It's different rules for men. We the king so there's some things y'all might not wanna do, [but] it gotta get done. I just can't do what you want me to do. I just can't."

I'm a fan of DJ Khaled's work, and it's unclear whether his thinking has changed since this interview. However, the attitude he displays here isn't unique. The belief that there are different rules for men and women is a stubborn ideology, and when men (and women) buy into this thinking, change becomes elusive and nearly impossible. There aren't different rules for men and women. And we shouldn't buy into an idea that somehow women are subordinate because these fictitious rules imply that men are superior. If we believe in a double standard, in a set of rules that implies the superiority of men just because they are male, this double standard belief can continue to perpetuate the various kinds of abuse (psychological, physical, spiritual, and emotional) that women have experienced and continue to experience at the hands of men.

Many men have bought into a false idea of what it means to be a man. This false idea leads to feelings of entitlement, and that contributes to chauvinistic behavior that is detrimental to men, and especially to women. I wrote this book to help men and women understand how this all goes back to the Dog, and to help men learn how to master it.

It may seem strange that I also wrote this book for women, but I did because they are on the receiving end of much of the damage the Dog does, and I want them to understand how to deal with the Dog too. Ladies, we are all in this together, and I wish I could tell you that every man in your life is going to do the work and is automatically going to get it together, but that's just not true. I pray this book will motivate and inspire them to become better, but while that process is under way, I don't want you to be in the dark. I want to tell you the truth as I see it as a way to help you deal with the Dog too.

I wrote the book *The Wait* with my wife, Meagan. It is a countercultural book about relationships that encourages readers to value delayed gratification over instant gratification, primarily by waiting for sex until marriage. In that book, we talk about the incidents in our personal lives that led us to make a vow of celibacy even before we started dating each other and about the benefits we experienced in our life as we waited. We had no idea the book would strike such a strong chord with men and women all around the world. I decided to wait while I was still single, many years before I ever met Meagan, because I didn't want to be preaching one thing and doing another. Navigating life in Hollywood as a single, celibate, high-powered executive and preacher definitely came with its set of challenges; however, it ultimately gave me experience and credibility with how to master the Dog. The practice of consistently sacrificing my personal desire for sex, managing my own lust for power, and committing to the process of personal success as a single man has helped me navigate the challenges of the Dog as a married man. This experience has given me the credibility to equip men and women with tools to become more successful in these areas. That journey laid the foundation for me to write this book.

Since *The Wait* was published, women from all over the world have contacted me, telling me they are tired of the pain men cause when they say one thing and do another. They have also told me they are sick of men telling them "what they need to know about men" without having those same men be challenged to take responsibility for their actions. More than once, I've been asked, "DeVon, when are men going to step up?"

Even though Maria Shriver's prompting was compelling, I finally decided to write this book because I was tired of seeing the hurt in women's eyes when they talk about the pain, anger, humiliation, and devastation men have caused them because so many men haven't or won't commit to the process of controlling their lust. I realized it was time to write this book when I saw that there are men out there who are legitimately struggling with how to become better men, yet have almost no guidance on how to do so.

I don't write this from a perspective of some self-righteous master. I'm no exception to any of the difficult truths I tackle in this book. Even though I'm a faithfully and happily married man for six years now, I have a Dog within me, too. If I try to act like my standing as a man of faith and a man in Hollywood makes me immune to my own lust, I am setting myself up for destruction, and I increase the chances that I will one day see the hurt in my wife's eyes. Every single day I have to work at accepting, training, and mastering the Dog so that it doesn't get the best of me. It's some of the hardest yet most rewarding work I've ever done. All men are vulnerable to the Dog. If I act like I'm not, pride will make me its victim.

It's not just me, either. All over the world, good, well-intentioned men have the potential to be ruined by the Dog. Why? Because the Dog that remains unacknowledged, undisciplined, and untrained is dangerous.

Training the Dog is not easy, but it can be done. Academy Award winner Jamie Foxx tells a story about how the Dog within him was out of control before the Oscars in 2005 when he was up for Best Actor for playing Ray Charles in *Ray*. In an interview with Howard Stern on May 23, 2017, he said, "I'm having such a good time, and I'm not knowing I'm f**king up, I mean I'm drinking, I'm doing every f**king thing you could possibly imagine or not and then I get a call."

The call was from none other than Oprah Winfrey, and she was not pleased. In the interview with Stern, Foxx said that Oprah told him, "You're blowing it, Jamie Foxx. All of this gallivanting and all this kind of sh*t, that's not what you want to do. I want to take you somewhere. Make you understand the significance of what you're doing."

He said that Oprah took him to a gathering at Quincy Jones's home in the Hollywood Hills, where some of the top black actors from the 1960s and '70s were waiting to do something like an intervention. Among them was the legendary actor Sidney Poitier, who said to Jamie, "I want to give you one thing. I want to give you responsibility. When I saw your performance, it made me grow two inches."

The message they were sending was clear: *You have an opportunity, but also a responsibility. Don't screw it up.* Foxx says he was so moved, and so ashamed, that he wept.

He told Stern, "To this day, it's the most significant time in my life."

Oprah and those great men did something that is the key to getting the Dog under control: they appealed to the Master, and they succeeded in helping Foxx tame the Dog.

A USER'S MANUAL

The Truth About Men is a user's manual for both men and women, whether single or married, to help them become equipped with the necessary knowledge, insights, and tools to transform their lives.

Men, this book will give you the road map for how to unleash the Master within. It will help you get control of the Dog, become the man you were created to be, and give you the help you need to claim victory in every area of your life.

Women, this book will give you insight into men and give you a look behind the veil of manhood. With knowledge there is tremendous power, and this book will give you real-time understanding on navigating your personal and professional relationships with men more effectively. But I will go beyond that, and give you specific information on not only what you're up against, but also on how to prevail.

This book is to be used as a conversation and communication starter. Men and women spend too much time talking *at* one another and not enough time talking *with* one another.

Where there is no communication,
there can be no transformation.

My hope is that this book can be used as a powerful tool for personal and collective transformation for both men and women. Yet, this all starts with building and repairing effective communication. We have to start by first having honest conversations. Honesty isn't a sign of weakness but of strength. When we can admit we don't have it all together, that we're struggling to figure out how to deal with one another better and that we need help in the process, this is when positive change can take place. Communication is one of the main keys to effecting change.

Communication is also one of the key tools of effective training. I utilize the dog-training metaphor throughout the book not as a way to vilify or demonize men, but because I think of the metaphor as a transformational framework to introduce practical tips and tools that can lead to true freedom and personal success. In my own life I've seen the power of what training can do, and I know it can do the same for any man who has the courage to try it and any woman who has the desire to listen.

So, are men really dogs? No. But it's time we learn to stop acting like we are.

CHAPTER 1

BE(A)WARE OF THE DOG

I'm a dog, I'm a dog, I'm a dog, I'm a dog
Every dog has its day man, every dog.
—GUCCI MANE, "I'M A DOG"

Considering the natural lust of power so inherent in man,
I fear the thirst of power will prevail to oppress the people.
—GEORGE MASON, FROM HIS SPEECH AT THE VIRGINIA
RATIFYING CONVENTION, JUNE 4, 1788

It's time to come out of the dark. We can't relegate this issue to the sidelines any longer. I want you to be aware.

We've all seen those signs that say "Beware of Dog." My grandfather had one to warn neighbors about the two hunting dogs in his backyard. But I don't just want you to *be*ware of the Dog any longer, I want you to become *a*ware of it. Becoming aware of the problem is the crucial first step toward fixing it.

I want you to know exactly what the Dog is and what can be done about it, so throughout this book, I will function as your "Dog whisperer." I will use the dog-training metaphor throughout as a way to share practical methods and specific training tips on how to master the Dog.

There are many dog trainers around the world, and they all have different theories and methods on how to train a dog. These methods range from clicker training to positive reinforcement to dominance training. But there's no method called self-training, where a dog learns how to improve its behavior on its own. The training methods all require patience, persistence, commitment, and control, and they all require help from the outside. Similarly, it's very difficult for a man to be who he needs to be without the right woman in his life (whether that's a mother, wife, girlfriend, sister, aunt, cousin, etc.). Women can and do play a vital role in this process if a man allows it.

Let's be clear about something—a man's Dog can't be trained by anyone other than himself. He has sole responsibility for his actions and he has to do his own work. But if a man allows a woman into the process, then she can play a positive part in the training.

Before we can get deeper into the training, there are a few basics you need to know.

MAN'S BEST FRIEND?

If you're a dog lover, then at the onset you might be offended that I would equate the worst of men with man's best friend. But don't tune me out just yet. A dog is the metaphor I'm using to help articulate what's going on inside a man that contributes to bad behavior. It's very similar to Sigmund Freud's description of the id. According to Freud, the id is home to the body's basic instincts, particularly those involving sex and aggression. The id lacks logic and reason, is impulse-driven, and wants its needs to be satisfied immediately. An untrained dog behaves in a similar way, and that's why I've chosen to use it in this way.

No matter how adorable a dog may be, there is nothing cute about an untrained dog. In his book *Dog Training: Strategic Dog Training Tips for a Well-Behaved, Obedient, and Happy Dog*, dog trainer Michael Kenssington writes, "Everyone knows a dog who has full run of a house and follows no orders; dogs like these are disobedient and can even be dangerous. Taking a dog who does not know how to sit or stay to an off-leash park could put him and the other dogs and people there at risk . . ."

Men have an all-consuming drive within, and men are rarely taught how to discipline it. In that way, it's like having a powerful but untrained dog every moment, day and night. And the absence of honest conversation about this drive, the dearth of practical tips on how to deal with it, and the lack of accountability for its effects, is destroying men, women, and everything we care about. Because we don't understand what the Dog is and why its influence is so strong, we don't grasp the fact that it can be trained and tamed, and as a result men are surrendering to the Dog's demands far too often. That can make many men a liability to themselves, spouses, girlfriends, employers, and potentially everyone in their life, no matter how much they are cared about.

When men don't master the Dog, they are choosing to satisfy self-centered (lustful) desires above all else. This satisfaction can happen at the expense of fidelity, commitments, and integrity. Choosing to please "self" above everything and everyone else can make men dangerous, because we can end up inflicting pain, sometimes without even realizing it, on the very people who have come to love and depend on us.

THE DOG FIGHT

There are wars raging all across the world, yet one of the greatest rages inside every man. I call this the Dog Fight. Whether you're a man or a woman reading this, I need you to know that every man is in a tug-of-war between his spirit and his flesh. You've heard the well-known saying found in Matthew 26:41: "The spirit is indeed willing, but the flesh is weak." Inside every man there is a higher man—the love, aka the Master—where the spirit resides. The spirit in a man wants to do right, be faithful, love himself and those around him. Yet inside every man there's also a lower man—the lust, aka Dog—where the desires of the flesh reside. The Dog wants its needs met above all others, doesn't care about what's right or good, and doesn't care about the damage it causes. The Master and the Dog fight for control of each man. In order for men to be successful, they must learn to master the Dog. And while all men struggle with this, no man's battle with the Dog is the same.

Why are men this way? Were men created this way, or is it a direct result of sin or something else? I don't know the exact answer. Maybe it's God's way of keeping us humble. Maybe it's the result of our socialization or development up to this point, or maybe it's a combination of these factors. This is an age-old question. Instead of getting into an anthropological or theological discourse, I'm going to keep the focus practical, because there have been many times I've cried out in agony, "Why can't *it* go away? Why is it so hard to be the man I desperately want to be?" I think of the words of Paul from Romans 8:18–20 (The Message): ". . . I realize that I don't have what it takes. I can will it, but I can't do it. I decide to do good, but I don't really do it; I decide not to do bad, but then I do it anyway. My decisions, such as they are, don't result in actions. Something has gone wrong deep within me and gets the better of me every time."

A few years ago I was at a bachelor party for one of my best friends, and we were with a group of men of all ages. We sat down to eat at Mastro's Steakhouse in Beverly Hills, and it felt good to be in the company of a great brotherhood. As the evening progressed, the younger men in the group started asking the older men about the keys to a successful marriage. One of the older men said ominously, "*It* never goes away."

That "it" was the Dog Fight. That "it" was men's battle with lust. I was at the beginning of my marriage, so I was perplexed by what he was saying, and I prayed it wasn't true. But I've discovered he was telling the truth. Lust never goes away. It's our Achilles' heel.

Yet, there's hope. Most trainers agree that every dog must be trained, and even with differing perspectives on how to train dogs effectively there are a few key principles that most trainers agree with. My hope is that these principles help you master the Dog.

LOOK THE DOG IN THE EYE

It's important to look a dog in the eye as a way of acknowledging its presence. The same goes for the Dog within—we have to look it in the eye and confront it if we ever aspire to get control of it.

As I mentioned, the Dog is lust. Lust is powerful, persistent, and pervasive. Romance novelist Karen Marie Moning has written about it as follows: "Lust is a thing of the blood. Doesn't need head or heart." *Merriam-Webster* defines it this way:

lust

noun | \ 'lest \

1   a : pleasure, delight

    b : personal inclination : wish

2   usually intense or unbridled sexual desire : lasciviousness

3   a : an intense longing : craving

    b : enthusiasm, eagerness

If I were astronaut Jim Lovell looking down at our society from Apollo 13, I would have said, "Houston, we have a lust problem." In a blog post for AskMen.com, psychologist Dr. Gregory Jantz, author of the book *Battles Men Face: Strategies to Win the War Within*, writes that lust is dangerous. "The very temptations we [men] entertain for the sake of strengthening our perceived manhood only serve as the most dangerous of distractions. Giving in to a temptation can fill a void, but only in the short term. This sets the stage for chronic compulsions, entrapping good men in a vicious cycle of destructive behavior."

Taking it a step further, the French philosopher the Marquis de Sade said, "Lust is to the other passions what the nervous fluid is to life; it supports them all, lends strength to them all . . . ambition, cruelty, avarice, revenge, are all founded on lust." Amen. When lust goes unchecked, the worst is yet to come.

For example, look at the Facebook-Cambridge Analytica scandal, in which 87 million Facebook users had their data exposed. While Facebook has apologized and tried to take responsibility for the loophole Cambridge Analytica took advantage of, they are still complicit, as there have been multiple reports stating that they knew of the breach more than two years before it became public. Sandy Parakilas, a former Facebook employee who worked on the privacy side of the company, told the *New York Times*, "The people whose job is to protect the user always are fighting an uphill battle against the people whose job it is to make money for the company." This is just one example of how unchecked lust can take many forms—in this case the form of greed, and millions of people suffered as a result.

If you own a dog, you know that as devoted as that dog might be, its primary concern is pleasure. Any dog lives for dinnertime, treats, walks, belly scratches, and playing fetch. That's it. Dogs crave pleasure at any cost, and the Dog in men is the same.

Women, is the man in your life always seeking pleasure at the expense of honest conversation, real connection, and truthful commitment? A man whose main focus is his own pleasure has left the Dog in control, not the Master. If you're a woman and you find yourself in this circumstance with your man, read on. I'll give you tips on how to deal with this.

When lust rises up in a man, it's like a dog that's barking. It will not stop until it gets our attention. The Dog wants pleasure to satisfy its hunger. There's nothing wrong with pleasure, but we all need to find the balance between pleasure, responsibility, and sacrifice. As a man, I need to remember that not every circumstance is designed for my personal pleasure. It's important to learn the practice of sacrifice: giving up what I want in the moment for the greater good.

But when men consistently feed the Dog pleasure as soon as it barks, it creates a dependency similar to that of an addict. Then, when men can't have those pleasures met, they can become irritable, angry, and frustrated. When the pursuit of pleasure becomes the sole focus and when men surrender to their urges often enough, the Dog becomes dangerous. If a man follows this path long enough he risks getting to a place where he becomes so dependent on his desires being satisfied that he can feel entitled to having them satisfied whenever—and by whomever—he chooses.

Anything We Don't Confront, We Empower to Conquer Us

Arizona dog trainer Jake Buvala wrote a blog post "How You Might Be Accidentally Training Your Dog to Misbehave" and he gives this example to illustrate the dangers of ignoring a dog. "You put Lola out into the backyard," he says. "After a few minutes, she gets bored and starts barking at imaginary villains beyond the fence. You stick your head out the door, yelling at her to shut up. Well, well, well. Lola just discovered a surefire way to get you to come outside and relieve her loneliness. . . . To a bored dog who spends most of her time alone, even being yelled at for barking is more exciting than being ignored."

Ignorance isn't bliss when it comes to dealing with the Dog. Ignoring the Dog is a sure way to make it act up. Men, let's stop acting like it doesn't exist and do the work of admitting that we struggle. Let's admit that there's something inside of us that needs attention. As I've mentioned, we all struggle to varying degrees. Every man's struggle is different, but there's still a struggle. The first step toward victory is acknowledging we have a problem in this area.

Women, this is equally critical for you to be aware of. As they say on New York City subways and in airports around the country, "If you see something, say something." Don't ignore the Dog when you see it on display in the man in your life. What does Dogish behavior look like? It sometimes looks like male chauvinism, ego-maniacal behavior, consistent disregard for your feelings, or lying, cheating, or displaying "my way or the highway" behavior. Don't be in denial about what you see. If you see something isn't right, don't turn a blind eye.

But what if you're dealing with sexual harassment in the workplace, not just bad behavior in private? Should you say something? I like the way Oprah addressed this. One of her followers on Instagram lamented that "sometimes [you] have to find a way to deal with abuse because to not deal with it can leave you without a job, home, family." She lamented how she wished she "could believe #TimesUp but in my world it will never end." Oprah responded by saying, "You do what you can to make your life work. I was harassed for years in my 20s and said nothing because I KNEW for SURE I would have been not only fired, but blackballed in the news business. I also knew I won't be here taking this ___ forever. Hold on. Hang in. Do what you need to do to set yourself FREE!" Everyone's situation is different, and knowing how to respond to each situation requires consideration and thoughtfulness. Do I believe a woman should endure harassment? Absolutely not. However, because we don't live in an ideal world, and there are many men in power who can and do abuse that power, I do believe in the sentiment that Oprah expressed that dealing with harassment requires wisdom.

Yes, There's a Problem

There's also a wild, restless force that exists in men, and it's essential that we acknowledge it. As a young man, one of the best books I read on manhood was *Wild at Heart: Discovering the*

Secret of a Man's Soul by John Eldredge. In this wonderful book, Eldredge poetically and powerfully articulates the deep yearning in men for adventure. There's a passage where he speaks passionately about the explorer that resides in all men:

> *Deep in a man's heart are some fundamental questions that simply cannot be answered at the kitchen table. Who am I? What am I made of? What am I destined for? It is fear that keeps a man at home where things are neat and orderly* and under his control. *But the answers to his deepest questions are not to be found on television or in the refrigerator. . . . If a man is ever to find out who he is and what he's here for, he has got to take that journey for himself.*
>
> *He has got to get his heart back.*

I love this passage because I find it to be so true. As men, we are at our best when we're confident explorers, operating within our purpose with the faith to move fearlessly into the unknown. When we aren't doing this consistently we become restless, often without knowing it. It's this restlessness in our spirit that produces the feeling of being unfulfilled. This can actually make us more susceptible to the ways of the Dog.

Why? Because society has changed so much and yet the essence of whom we are as men hasn't. We no longer live in a time when exploring the wilderness is as easy as walking beyond the comforting glow of a frontier town's gaslights. I can place a satellite call from the summit of Everest; I can fly from New York to Dubai in less than thirteen hours. The world is smaller and probably more docile than ever, and part of every man mourns that, whether we know it or not.

Most of today's conquests are found working in an office, piloting a laptop and updating a spreadsheet. The mobile app Waze keeps us from getting pleasantly lost on back roads, while Amazon Prime delivers what we want shortly after we know we want it. We still ache to escape, seek adventure, and test our limits. I feel that same pull myself. As much as I love what I do, part of me longs to break away from my normal routine and just explore, to not worry about my work but just be free to be *myself*.

That conflict is a tricky thing for a man to deal with. I know I've had trouble. I've had many wonderful accomplishments. I run a successful production company, have a vibrant speaking career, appear regularly on TV, have more than a million followers on social media, and have published four books by the age of forty. But I still find myself consumed by the lust for more. One great achievement leads to the desire for another, and then another, and before I know it, I'm hooked on the chase. When that happens, nothing is enough, and as a result I don't feel good enough as a man. It's insidious, and it warps our perception of our self-worth.

I know I'm not alone. Many men have been told that the measure of a man is in his wealth, status, and achievements. We see what other men achieve in their lives, and despite ourselves we use that as a barometer for our worth. That's dangerous, because it puts the Dog in control. If the pleasure of one accomplishment isn't enough, the Dog barks and says, "I want more." When the Master isn't in charge, we seek pleasure for pleasure's sake. We feel inadequate. And if we don't have discipline and safeguards in place, we can become tempted to look for other forms of pleasure so we can feel powerful and enjoy a sense of conquest.

So look the Dog in the eye. But be aware! Most dog trainers agree that a dog will view sustained eye contact as a threat, and when a dog feels threatened it will push back. Men, the more you begin to look, the more likely it is the Dog will start to rebel. You might have thoughts in your head such as "I've got this" or "Whatever, I don't need this, I'm good." These thoughts might tempt you to shun any attempts at discipline or any attempts at learning to become better. Pay attention, and don't let the Dog win this fight.

Women, as you begin to look more closely at the Dog in men and stop turning a blind eye, expect that you'll meet with some resistance. Even a man who wants to master his Dog might get defensive when you start pointing out some of his bad behavior. That doesn't mean you should give up, though. Just understand and expect some potential defensiveness.

For both men and women, don't allow the rebellion or resistance you might get from the Dog to stop you from making "eye contact." Mastery requires observation and, at times, confrontation.

UNDERSTAND THE ENVIRONMENT

In a blog post titled "Factors Known to Influence a Dog's Behavior," professional dog trainer Adrienne Farricelli writes,

"The environment may play a big role in a dog's behavior." Lust is the root cause of the problems that men are experiencing, but no one is talking about it. Why? Part of the problem is that we live in an environment that is fueled by and profits off that lust.

From commercials and movies to TV shows and social media, there is a deliberate and calculated effort to entice lust, especially in men. In "Three Major Ways Advertising Attracts Straight Men," Paul Suggett, creative director for Starz Entertainment, says, "Sex sells. When it comes to beer, men are bombarded with images of scantily clad models holding cans of ice-cold lager, laughing at their jokes, finding them irresistible and also incredibly handsome. But it's men who drink the beer, so why do the women have the beer goggles on? And then there are those ads that portray women who are 'tens,' chasing nerdy guys and average Joes down the high street because they sprayed something slightly nice smelling under their smelly pits that morning. Yes, that happens. But for some reason, men look. And they buy. And they buy again."

The Geena Davis Institute on Gender in Media and J. Walter Thompson New York, an international advertising agency, recently co-published a study about the portrayal of women in media in conjunction with the University of Southern California. The study noted that, "Between 2006 and 2016 women were shown in sexually revealing clothing six times more than men."

In other words, pop culture objectifies women in order to turn them from people into objects of lust. It does this intentionally, because that drives profits. Dr. Susan Krauss Whitbourne, Professor Emerita of Psychological and Brain Sciences at the University of Massachusetts, Amherst, has shared her thoughts on the topic of media influence on the mind. As referenced in a blog post written by Annie Behnke titled "Media's Influence on the Objectification of Women," Dr. Whitbourne defines *objectification* as a term that "refers to a tendency to treat an individual not as a person with emotions and thoughts, but as a physical being or 'object.' In most cases, the term means thinking of the person . . . as a sexual object, there to provide pleasure to others."

Even hip-hop, which in recent years has become the dominant form of music in American culture, is dominated by messages of lust for drugs, women, sex, money, and fame. After seeing the movie *Straight Outta Compton*, one of my industry associates and great filmmaker Ava DuVernay tweeted, "To be a woman who loves hip hop at times is to be in love with your abuser. Because the music was and is that. And yet the culture is ours."

As a producer in Hollywood and a growing fixture in media, I know there is more we can do as a community to create positive change. This is the other side of the #MeToo and #TimesUp coin that we must address: *content*. In addition to putting an end to sexual harassment, we also must look at the content we produce and its role in fostering negative behavior in young boys that carries on into manhood. It's time for those of us in the entertainment industry to take greater responsibility for the content we create, and do this in conjunction with the other initiatives being enacted to stop sexual harassment.

Women Manage the Environment Better Than Men

Lust is, of all the frailties of our nature,

what most we ought to fear; the headstrong beast

rushes along, impatient of the course;

nor hears the rider's call, nor feels the rein.

—NICHOLAS ROWE, FROM *THE ROYAL CONVERT*

Do women deal with lust? Absolutely. Lust is not a challenge exclusive to men. However, men have a greater challenge dealing with the issues lust presents. Dr. John Lydon from McGill University in Montréal, Canada, conducted a "lust experiment." As detailed in *ScienceDaily*, this lust experiment involved 724 men and women in relationships. They were monitored for how they responded to an attractive person. College-aged women and men in committed relationships were part of the seven laboratory experiments conducted to see how they acted when another attractive person was in the process.

In one of the studies, half of the unsuspecting men were introduced to a "single" and attractive flirtatious woman while the other half met a woman who was "unavailable" and ignored them. The women in the experiment were put in a similar situation. Right after this, they were asked to answer some questions about how they would react if their significant other had done something that bothered them. Men who met the attractive single woman were about 12 percent less likely to forgive their significant other while the women who were put into the same situation were about 17.5 percent more likely to forgive.

"One interpretation of these studies is that men are unable to ward off temptation. We do not subscribe to this. Instead, we believe men simply interpret these interactions differently than women do . . . We think that if men believed an attractive, available woman was a threat to their relationship, they might try to protect that relationship." Dr. Lydon concluded that "men give into sexual temptation easier than women," and that "Women have been socialized to be wary of the advances of attractive men."

Most women—even the ones reading this—will admit that they too have lustful thoughts, just like men do. Yet I agree with the findings of this study; in my experience, men have more difficulty in dealing with it. In my experience, women consistently exercise a greater deal of control over lust than men do.

KNOW THE BREED

The breed of a dog significantly influences its behavior. The World Canine Organization recognizes 344 different breeds of dogs. Each one comes with certain behavioral characteristics, and sometimes dog owners are unsuccessful in training their dogs because they neglect to understand the history and typical traits of their dog and don't tailor the training specifically to the breed.

I want you to consider the Dog in men as a breed unto itself. Here are some of the characteristics of this breed and how it operates so you know what you need to be aware of.

The Dog Is Selfish and Impulsive

The Dog only cares about itself. It's interested in getting its needs met at any cost, and it doesn't want to be disciplined. Don't get fooled into believing for one second that the Dog has your best interests at heart. That selfishness leads to impulsive, terrible decisions. The Dog doesn't stop to consider commitments to family, marriage, or even the church. When it's empowered, it will immediately seek to satisfy its hunger for money, power, fame, or sex—even if that means violating everything men hold dear. It hungers for instant gratification. Only after it's done will a man feel remorse, and by then, it could be too late.

For women, be careful if the man you're dealing with consistently puts his needs and wants before yours. This is a telltale sign that the Dog is in control. True love is built on sacrifice and that sacrifice often means putting others' needs above your own. If the man you're dealing with doesn't do this, take note.

The Dog Is Manipulative

The Dog is a danger because it can cause men to become manipulative, self-serving, controlling, callous, dismissive, and deceptive.

Chris Rock did an interview where he acknowledged the Dog destroyed his marriage. "I was a piece of sh*t," he said, adding that he felt he could cheat on his wife because he was the famous breadwinner in the family. "That's bullsh*t," he admitted. "Your significant other, if they really love you, has a high opinion of you. And you let them down." The Dog causes men to become manipulative, and when it's in control, it can manipulate the man into thinking certain actions—like cheating—are acceptable, when they never are.

Ladies, always put your self-worth and well-being over your desire to have a man in your life. What I mean is that you can be respected *and* have the right person at the same time. It's not an either-or decision. However, when your desire to have a man in your life is greater than your desire to be respected, you can find yourself in a situation where you are inadvertently manipulated by a man who is controlled by the Dog. The Dog in a man can sniff out your weakness and exploit it for his gain. If you are experiencing behavior from him that makes you feel less than who you know you are, that chips away at your self-esteem, then it's time to see things as they really are and confront the situation or leave outright. Also, don't just resign yourself to dealing with the Dog because you believe this is the only way to have a man in your life. It's just not true. Can it be difficult to find the right man? Definitely. Is it worth being in a situation with a man that eats away at your self-esteem because you feel it's the best you can do? Never.

The Dog Likes to Behave Differently Outside the House

Public success isn't personal success. As men, we can't just focus on succeeding publicly; we must also succeed personally. History is filled with examples of men who were public successes and personal failures. Integrity is not what we do when others are watching; it's what we do when no one else is around. Real success begins when we are successful personally, and that manifests in our public lives. It's not the other way around. Too many men want the public to admire the Master while we allow the Dog to run wild behind closed doors.

Don't delude yourself into thinking you can let the Master handle your public life while the Dog goes berserk behind the scenes. That's the dynamic that's brought down so many prominent men. The days when a man could maintain a respectable public facade but be the opposite behind the scenes are over.

My brothers, there's always a reckoning. *Always.* That was true even before #MeToo. We can't live like this anymore. There is a difference between public and personal success; they do not draw water from the same well. We can't just lead publicly. We must do so personally, too.

For women, don't be more impressed with a man's public success than you are with his personal success. It's easy to put on a show in public, but the true test is what happens in private. So many men want to woo you publicly then give you hell privately. See how they treat others in private, when no one else is looking. See how they treat their family, especially their mother, and honestly assess what you see. Does his public persona match who he is privately? If not, steer clear. Who he is privately is who he truly is.

The Dog Likes to Play (and Too Often Women Have Been the Toys)

One of the most common unhealthy forms of male conquest is the dogged pursuit of women. *Womanizing* is defined as pursuing or courting women habitually. By this definition more men are womanizers than any of us would like to admit. But let's be honest, men: There's a thrill to pursuing a woman. When and if you win her, you feel powerful, at least for a while. Then the feeling fades and you want that thrill again, so you find yourself doing it again with another woman, even though you're in a committed relationship or dating a woman who thinks you're exclusive. But in your mind, you're only exclusive until you spot the next woman you want to track down.

This is a destructive pattern. The Dog in you wants to play, and too often its most desired toy is women. The Dog can get you to a place where you don't view women as the dynamic human beings they truly are and you see them only as objects of your personal and oftentimes sexual conquest. Wake up!

There are not enough women to fill the void men have in their souls. You could have all the women in the world and still not be happy. To placate that need for conquest in a healthy way, we must turn our pursuit within. The challenge for all men is to satisfy our innate hunger for exploration, risk, and conquest in healthy ways that do not disrupt our character, integrity, and peace.

This is an important truth for women to know, especially single women. Don't unknowingly allow yourself to be part of a man's conquest. Dating isn't a perfect science, and you might date someone who is sincere, and still find the relationship doesn't work out. That's okay. But it's not okay to be in the dark about a man's intentions, where you think something more significant is happening than he does. This is how you can end up as collateral damage in a man's desire for conquest.

One of the best ways to combat this is to *get out of the gray area*. Men who have the Dog in control love to play in the gray because that's where the shadows are. You get out of the gray by asking a man direct questions about his intentions and seeking out direct, clear answers. Don't assume anything about his intentions or draw any conclusions that haven't been confirmed by direct questioning. I've seen it time and again— women making the wrong assumption about where they were with a man. In the end, it only costs them. Assumptions keep you in the gray; answers take you into the light.

The Dog doesn't want to come into the light, so if you don't ask a man a direct question, then more than likely he won't give you a direct answer. Don't be afraid to know the truth about whom you're dealing with.

The same goes for married women—don't be afraid to find out what's going on with your husband. Open and honest communication is essential for a successful relationship and marriage. Married men can hide in the gray area too, and the gray area is a danger zone for your marriage. Many times, a wife assumes her husband is okay, yet she never takes the time to really ask him how he's doing, what might be stressing him out, or even what's concerning him the most. A man doesn't feel like his wife is in touch with what he's going through and he doesn't quite know if it's safe to express his true feelings. This can lead him to subconsciously—and sometimes consciously—disconnecting and finding relief in feeding the Dog. He may be committed to the marriage, but he's still privately struggling. Women, turn on the light. Get out of that gray area. Check in on your husband regularly. Ask him how he's really doing and don't just settle for surface answers. Men need you to check in more than they may ever express. If you suspect he's disconnecting or disconnected, don't be afraid to ask why.

One of the keys to helping facilitate successful inquiries and communication is *tone*. Men have a need to be and feel respected. I've seen many men turn off conversations they desperately needed to have because of the tone of voice their wife or girlfriend used to approach them. They got defensive and shut down. You can talk to your man while still being loving, caring, and considerate, and even firm without being condescending, belittling, or negative. Knowledge is power when it comes to dealing with the Dog. You've got to know the truth, so monitor your tone, yet don't be afraid to ask.

Men, it cuts both ways. Be mindful of your tone as well. Women need the same respect we do. Sometimes the Dog can make us feel frustrated and angry because it feels like it's not being satisfied. This dissatisfaction can come through when you're short-tempered, loud, or even angry toward the woman in your life. When you speak to her in a tone that is aggressive and inconsistent with the love you have for her, you run the risk of pushing her away and potentially inflicting emotional pain that you don't intend. Be mindful of using a tone that is consistent with the love you have for her, even when you might be in the midst of an argument or disagreement. This will contribute to more successful communication with her.

Lastly, because men have often been conditioned to be the leader in a relationship, we sometimes can mistake leadership for a dictatorship. We can sometimes take the position of "because I said so" when the woman in our life challenges us by not agreeing with what we say or how we want to do something. Remember, the best leaders lead by love and example, not by dictates, domination, and chauvinism. We need to hear what she has to say, and many times I've found that the way I want to do things isn't the best way to do them. When I listen to my wife and take heed of her counsel, the result is much better than what I would have done without it. Value and seek out input from the woman in your life. You are in each other's lives to make each other better.

The Dog Doesn't Disappear When You Fall in Love or Say "I Do"

I was so upset when I discovered this! I love my wife with all my heart, mind, body, and soul. That being said, I'd be lying if I said I've never had a lustful thought about another woman while we've been married. I'll never forget how right after we got married, I thought, *Amen, I'll never have to deal with the Dog again.*

Wrong! The nuptials only put the Dog to sleep. When it woke up, these lustful thoughts came upon me and I was angry. I didn't have a need, want, or desire for another woman *at all*, yet somehow the Dog would howl anyway. Anger turned to guilt, then to shame, and then to frustration. I began to ask, "What's wrong with me?"

Many men get frustrated when they discover that the Dog is still there after they fall in love or get married, and they're surprised and upset that they still have to manage their lustful feelings. But all men deal with this. I've come to learn that lust is way more powerful than I ever understood, and it can be enticed even against our will. Take Instagram, for example. How many times have you been scrolling through your feed when a picture of an attractive woman comes up and instantly the Dog starts to bark? What this has caused me to realize is that the Dog can't be eliminated—only trained, controlled, and mastered.

For married women, just because the Dog didn't disappear when your man said "I do" doesn't mean he has eyes for another woman, finds you less attractive, or even desires to be with someone else. I know many married men who love their wives and still acknowledge the presence of the Dog. Don't let this upset or anger you. My hope is that by letting you know the truth—that every man has the same problem and there's nothing wrong with him—you will be better equipped to deal with it.

The Dog Wants Sex All the Time (Don't Be Alarmed)

The Dog wants sex however and whenever it can get it! Men's seemingly nonstop drive for sex is one of the things that makes mastering the Dog so difficult. That's why I'm breaking down these truths—so that you have the necessary tools to identify what's happening and develop a strategy for success. Sometimes the Dog in you starts to howl and that deep desire for sex comes on you (in other words, you get horny), but it's not the right time, place, or person.

Billy Crystal has a famous line in the movie *City Slickers*: "Women need a reason to have sex. Men just need a place." That's true. And when that happens, sometimes you literally have to talk to the Dog and command: "Sit! Stay!"

But putting a lid on our rampaging libido isn't like flipping a switch. It takes hard, consistent work. You don't get a fit, healthy body by eating one salad and putting in a week of sessions on the treadmill; you have to work out and eat right consistently before you see results—for years before it becomes a way of life. The rewards are worth the work, but there is never a time when you will be able to say "Hey, this is easy." Managing your sex drive works the same way. It takes time, practice, and discipline, but it can be done.

For single women, this is an area where you can avoid falling into a trap. Sex is addictive, and when you have sex with a man who has devoted hundreds of hours of practice over the course of his life to having sex, that man can use his desire to have sex and his proficiency at having sex to get you hooked.

This is why I recommend waiting for sex until marriage, or at least as long as you possibly can. Waiting for sex will help you discern if this man is really interested in you or if the Dog just wants your body.

After *The Wait* came out, Meagan and I were grateful to be guests on Oprah's *Super Soul Sunday* to talk about celibacy, marriage, and a lot more. During that conversation, I told Oprah that I could predict when someone would be unfaithful after marriage. I said, "If I had no discipline in sex before marriage, I will have no discipline in sex after marriage."

If we constantly let the Dog run loose in our dating life, why would we be able to just magically put that Dog back on the leash after we pledge ourselves to one woman? A tragic number of marriages end because of infidelity—about fifteen percent, according to U.K.-based Co-operative Legal Services—because so many men *don't* discipline the Dog before they get serious with a woman. One of the reasons I believe there's so much infidelity and the divorce rate is so high is because as men, we don't focus on rigorous discipline in our dating/sex life before marriage. Those bad habits follow us into marriage.

The habits we have before entering into a committed relationship can determine our behavior after we're in that relationship. That's why it was so important that Meagan and I remained celibate before we got married. I felt that employing that kind of sexual discipline before we walked down the aisle would help give me a better chance to be a faithful husband. While I have found that to be true, I still have to invest daily effort in keeping my Dog on the leash.

ENOUGH IS ENOUGH: TAKE CONTROL

Part of being aware of the Dog is recognizing what can happen if the Dog goes unchecked. Every dog owner must make the decision to be in charge and take control of the dog. It all starts in the mind. Some of the nicest dog owners can be the worst at training dogs because they don't make the decision to take charge of the situation, even once it's gotten out of hand.

Lust is so out of control within men that even as I write this book, I can't write fast enough to keep up with all the news that keeps breaking around this subject. I've already mentioned the names of many of the men who've been publicly brought down by scandals over sexual harassment and assault. But one recent piece of news in particular got me so fired up, I have to mention it. I've always been an admirer of Tony Robbins and the self-help empire he's built. Recently he caught a wave of backlash for his comments about the #MeToo movement. At his Unleash the Power Within event in San Jose, he said, "If you use the #MeToo movement to try to get significance and certainty by attacking and destroying someone else, you haven't grown an ounce." In other words, he was insinuating that women were speaking out against men who had hurt them for selfish reasons, hoping to lift themselves up by tearing others down. He has since apologized, saying, "[S]ometimes the teacher has to become the student and it is clear that I still have much to learn."

But he said something else during the San Jose event that was also upsetting to me. He said he was speaking with a male CEO who had a job opening and there was an attractive woman who was more qualified than the male candidates. But because of the CEO's trepidation about the #MeToo movement, he wouldn't hire the attractive, qualified female candidate.

This is a problem we must confront. First, there is so much misunderstanding about what the movement is about. #MeToo and #TimesUp are not the "gotcha" police looking to bring down men for the sake of bringing them down. They are vehicles for women who have been legitimately assaulted and/or harassed to have support and a voice. So the idea that a male CEO wouldn't hire a woman because of her sex says more about the man's insecurity than it does about the movement itself.

Secondly, I wonder why he didn't challenge the CEO on his conclusion to not hire the best person for the job, even if that was an attractive woman. As he himself has said, "Let fear be a counselor and not a jailer."

Enough is enough. As men, we have to do our work and not be afraid of the necessary change that these movements are bringing to bear.

Sexual harassment and assault is an epidemic, and has been for longer than anyone wants to admit. The only thing that's different now is that women are no longer suffering in silence, and now these incidents are finally getting publicity. And with that publicity, the world is now seeing the prevalence of what I call *the Beast*.

The Beast is the Dog at his worst—truthfully, men at *their* worst. The Beast is lust set loose without any restraint or morality, willing to do *anything* to satisfy a man's desire for sex, domination, and power, even if that means using violence. The Dog becomes a Beast when a man will stop at nothing to have his urges met. Men who don't control the Beast court destruction.

Not all men have bad intentions. Most men want to be loving and honorable. But wanting that isn't enough. Intentions aren't enough. When men don't exercise control over the Dog, there is a risk of succumbing to the Beast and laying waste to everything good, not only in our lives but also the lives of so many others.

The trail of carnage left by the Beast can be seen from the White House to the campuses of the most prestigious universities in the country. Take the "pig roast" story that came out of Cornell University. The Ivy League school's Zeta Beta Tau fraternity was handed a two-year probation after it held a degrading contest in which new members would earn points each time they slept with a different woman—and the member who had sex with the woman who weighed the most would earn "bonus" points.

That is the Beast in action. It turns women into humiliated victims and men into primitive, sometimes criminal, creatures who couldn't be further removed from who we were created to be. Simply:

The Dog becomes a Beast when a man becomes physically, emotionally, spiritually, or psychologically violent to satisfy his lust.

Let's define *sexual assault* and *sexual harassment*. The U.S. Department of Justice defines sexual assault as "Any type of sexual contact or behavior that occurs without the explicit consent of the recipient." The U.S. Equal Employment Opportunity Commission (EEOC) defines sexual harassment as "Unwelcome sexual advances, requests for sexual favors, and other verbal or physical conduct of a sexual nature . . . when this conduct explicitly or implicitly affects an individual's employment, unreasonably interferes with an individual's work performance, or creates an intimidating, hostile, or offensive work environment."*

When the Dog becomes the Beast, men become capable of terrible things, including sexual assault and sexual harassment. Debris from the Beast's rampages litters our society everywhere we look, and the victims are usually women and children. When lust turns to harassment, assault, or acts of perversion and violence, the Beast is free, and the damage that results can be horrific. Here are a few statistics that blew me away:

- According to a 2017 poll conducted by MSN, about 1 in 3 people (31%) in the U.S. admit to being sexually harassed at work. Seventy-three percent of women who had been sexually harassed at work said they never reported it.
- According to *Business Insider*'s Lauren Lyons Cole, companies are collectively paying more than $2 billion an-

---

* U.S. Equal Employment Opportunity Commission, "Facts About Sexual Harassment," https://www.eeoc.gov/eeoc/publications/fs-sex.cfm.

nually in employee practices liability insurance (EPLI) to protect against the financial risk of sexual harassment.

- In the same *Business Insider* piece that details the results of the MSN poll, New Jersey employment lawyer Stephanie Gironda said, "Claims are so common now that it's more or less part of the cost of doing business." The majority of these claims are women reporting harassment by men.

When it comes to this issue of control, the question of "why" persists. Why do so many men seemingly have no control and just allow the Dog to become a Beast? We have all been shocked by the pervasiveness of harassment and by the identities of the perpetrators. I have former colleagues and associates who have been accused of sexual harassment and have subsequently lost their jobs. I was shocked, because these men never appeared to be anything less than respectful in public. Even now, it's hard to believe that they showed one side of themselves publicly while the Beast was doing something completely different in private.

Why do some men who are so successful in their careers still have such a blind spot to their own negative behavior? Why can't some men control the Dog and cage the Beast? Even if you haven't allowed the Dog to become the Beast (yet), why does some negative behavior feel out of your control?

Explanation, Rationalization, and Normalization

Rationalization: Allowing my mind to find reason to excuse
what my spirit knows is wrong.

—BRUCE EAMON BROWN, *1001 MOTIVATIONAL MESSAGES*
AND QUOTATIONS FOR ATHLETES AND COACHES

We have an internal alarm system that helps us distinguish right from wrong. Romans 2:15 says that right and wrong are already written in our hearts at birth. We have an inherent sense of behavior that's in bounds and out of bounds. So I believe that when we commit offenses that violate this innate sense of right and wrong, our internal alarm system goes off in our spirit, screaming, "This is wrong!" That alarm is so strong that we can't ignore it. We hear it and it hurts, because we know we did something we shouldn't have done.

However, the guilt and shame can be so great that instead of owning up to our behavior and putting ourselves on a path to address its root cause, we instead steer ourselves into a three-part process of *explanation*, *rationalization*, and *normalization*. It's this cycle that makes terrible acts seem excusable, then acceptable, and finally inevitable. I'll walk you through each stage and then explain how each one empowers the Beast.

Explanation is when you list the factors that led to the negative behavior that is disrupting your spirit. For example, let's say a man watched pornography, and after he did, he felt guilty and ashamed. Or he went out on a date with a woman, both got drunk, and had sex. Afterward, he didn't feel right about the encounter. Explanation helps sort through the facts. In the case of watching pornography the facts were:

- He was alone.
- He was stressed out.
- He was horny.

In the case of the date and the drunken sex, the facts were:

- He was feeling lonely.
- They had a good time together.
- He went to her house or she came over to his place.
- They both had been drinking.

Now that the facts are laid out, explanation by itself doesn't have to be a problem. The problem comes when that man finds himself going to the next stage to turn off the alarm bells of guilt and shame: rationalization.

Rationalization occurs when we reframe negative behavior as fair, just, or acceptable. Rationalization puts us at the top of a slippery slope, because we can tell ourselves comforting lies that justify our actions, and by so doing, dodge responsibility for them. In the case of watching pornography the rationalizations are:

- Nobody was hurt.
- It's okay to feel good.
- Nobody else was around.

In the case of the date and sex the rationalizations are:

- "We both were drunk and she wanted it as badly as I did."
- "She knew what time it was. It just happened."
- "She knew what I wanted when she went out with me."

When our actions are inconsistent with what we believe about our character, we rationalize the bad behavior so we don't have to feel bad about ourselves. As a result, we begin to deny the guilt or remorse associated with the behavior. Then we justify this behavior with statements like, "It's just the way men are," "Boys will be boys," and "She knows I've gotta have it." The rationalizations silence the alarm.

When we engage in this kind of dangerous rationalization often enough, we can become immune to guilt and remorse. That leads to normalization.

Normalization is when harmful, lustful behavior becomes a normal part of a man's life. The internal alarm system breaks. The man's desire to be aware of negative and potentially destructive behavior diminishes because the guilt and remorse formerly associated with that behavior are gone. Behavior that would have been repulsive to the man has now become habitual, even incorporated into his day-to-day life.

Many men fall into this process even when the Dog hasn't become the Beast. As I mentioned earlier, Chris Rock acknowledged that the Dog destroyed his marriage of eighteen years. On tour for his stand-up show *Alimony*, he admitted to cheating on his wife with three other women. In a follow-up interview with *Rolling Stone*, he said he rationalized his cheating because he felt he could get away with it because he was the family's breadwinner. So the cheating became rationalized, and once rationalized, it became a normalized part of his life until eventually he was forced to face the consequences. This is the vicious cycle that many men fall into. Men, consider this:

Have you normalized behavior that you know is destructive and inconsistent with who you profess to be? For women reading this: Have you experienced this type of normalized behavior with a man?

In its most extreme form, this process corrupts the spirit of good men, transforming them into Beasts. This is how we get serial sexual harassers. With their vast professional power, the more these men indulge the Beast within without consequences, the more they feel the right to conscience-free pleasuring whenever—and with whomever—they choose. That's how the Beast can terrorize so many.

Guilt, remorse, and shame are *healthy* responses to doing something harmful to ourselves or others. Anesthetizing ourselves to our internal alarm system sets us up for a devastating fall.

Challenging anything unhealthy in our life that has become normalized is a necessary step to taking control. The effectiveness of this training rests with the decision to take control, individually and collectively. For both men and women, I urge you to take full control of your life and actions. Men, take control by choosing to commit to the training process and no longer being satisfied with allowing lust to run wild.

Ladies, there are no doubt situations you have been in where a man took away your control and there was nothing you could do about it. I pray for your healing and restoration. I also pray that every man who forcefully took away your control (physically, emotionally, mentally, spiritually) will reap exactly what he has sown. Women, I want you to take control over whatever is within your power. Commit to applying this knowledge for your good.

FOR MEN: ARE YOU ACTING LIKE THE DOG?

There are telltale signs that show whether the Dog or Master is in control.

This is an assessment that will show you where you are today. Answer yes or no to these questions to discover whether you're more Dog or Master right now.

1. If you're single: When you go out on a date, is sex your only objective?

2. If you're single: Would you or have you stopped dating a woman because she wanted to wait until marriage for sex?

3. If you're single: Do you intentionally keep the women you're dating from finding out about each other?

4. If you're single: Do you regularly have one-night stands?

5. Married or Single: Have you cheated or are you currently cheating on your spouse or girlfriend?

6. Married or Single: Do you watch pornography regularly?

7. Married or Single: Do you make excuses for buddies who harass or cheat?

8. Married or Single: Are you primarily focused on making money more than anything else?

9. Married or Single: Do you portray an image in front of other men just to be accepted?

If you answered Yes to more than one of these questions, the Dog is loose.

FOR WOMEN: ARE YOU DEALING WITH THE DOG?

1. If you're single: When you go out on a date, is sex your date's main objective?

2. If you're single: Has someone stopped dating you because you wanted to wait for sex until marriage?

3. If you're single: Does the man you're dating give you vague answers every time you ask direct questions?

4. If you're single: Do you regularly have one-night stands?

5. Married or Single: Do you suspect your spouse or boyfriend is currently cheating on you?

6. Married or Single: Does the man you're with watch pornography regularly?

7. Married or Single: Does the man you're with hang out with other men who are known harassers or cheaters?

8. Married or Single: Is the man you're with primarily focused on making money more than anything else?

9. Married or Single: Do you see the man you're with portray an image in front of other men just to be accepted that's different from the image he portrays in front of you?

If you answered Yes to more than one of these questions, you are dealing with the Dog more than you are dealing with the Master.

CHAPTER 2

ACCEPT THE DOG

I'm a dog . . . and you know it.
—YO GOTTI, "DOGG"

A wound that goes unacknowledged and unwept is a wound
that cannot heal.
—JOHN ELDREDGE, *WILD AT HEART*

Good intentions aren't enough to tame the Dog. There have been times in my life when the Master wasn't in control and the Dog was running wild. I found myself only caring about what I wanted, and I hurt some women by not being honest about my intentions and by putting the fulfillment of my desires above theirs. If someone had told me at that time "You're acting like a dog," I would have denied it, because I was ignoring the Dog in me.

One of the keys to success is *acceptance*. Accept the Dog. It's important for a man to accept that no matter how faithful or well-intentioned he might be, there is still a Dog inside of him. There's no getting rid of it, no leaving it at the Humane Society after hours in a box with "Please take care of this good boy" scrawled on it with a Sharpie. There is an eternal war going on in every man between the Master and the Dog—between our higher self and our lower, animal self—and no man is an exception, including me.

It can be difficult for some men to accept that we all have a Dog. Remember, the Dog is just a metaphor for lust. For some, admitting they have a lust problem feels like the equivalent of admitting that you have an STD or some other embarrassing condition they don't want anyone to know about. But remaining in denial can lead to potential peril, as we've already seen. Denial is a psychological trick that has dire consequences. Remember, the Dog that isn't acknowledged will act out and get the attention it is seeking one way or another, maybe even turning into the Beast. A man reading this can try to trick himself into believing what I'm saying is a bunch of mumbo jumbo. However, denial only empowers the lust within to come out in ways that might shock you.

Yes, acceptance can be scary. With acceptance comes vulnerability and responsibility. It's terrifying for men to admit that there's something inside us waging a war against the man we aspire to be. However, I encourage acceptance because doing so will help any man embrace the need for personal responsibility. Anything we accept, we have to take responsibility for dealing with. Accept the Dog so it can be dealt with, instead of letting it deal with you.

On my personal journey, I had to accept that I had a Dog within me, and that wasn't easy. I didn't want to see myself that way. I wanted to think I was the exception, not the rule. But no man is perfect, including me. Even now, publicly admitting that I have lust within me is difficult. But it's helpful. As I accept the Dog within me, it helps me accept a sobering reality: if I don't do my work, I have the potential to be unfaithful, act against my vows, and be something other than the man I want to be.

That admission makes me humble. It makes me cautious. It makes me not take my own strength or virtue for granted. It also keeps me from acting "holier than thou." Among men, there's so much public judgment, finger-pointing, and self-righteousness when it comes to sex and infidelity. All men know that letting the Dog out is easier than any of us cares to admit.

I had to accept my own weakness before I could focus on how to become stronger. I had to admit that I needed to manage what I felt going on in my spirit. I discovered secrets to taming, training, and controlling the Dog, and in this discovery true strength was revealed.

Any man can learn to bench-press three hundred pounds in the gym, but learning to manage lust requires an entirely different level of strength.

FEEL THE URGE

> Who is a hero? He who conquers his urges.
> —THE TALMUD

To accept the Dog, it's important to feel the urges it creates within us. Those urges are the Dog barking. They're the feel-

ing of being horny, greedy, envious, and prideful. Do not ignore
the barking. Instead, hear it. Feel the urge and accept that it is
there. Don't suppress the urge or pretend it doesn't exist. Suppressing urges is the surest way for the Dog to win.

Anything that we suppress eventually gets expressed in
unhealthy ways.

When we suppress something, it builds up. If you're a dog
owner and your dog is barking and no one acknowledges it,
eventually it gets angry and rips apart your couch. That's its
way of saying, "See? Don't ignore me." When we suppress our
urges, they don't go away; they persist. The urges that persist
are the urges that insist on being addressed. Merissa Bury, a
writer and marketing specialist, wrote the following in a piece
for the *HuffPost*: "Sex. One of the greatest motivational forces
in life. Our sexual impulses control so much of what we do,
how we act, and the choices we make. But if not properly har-
nessed, they can lead to great destruction."

I've been in the church my whole life and I can say that no
one—and I mean *no one*—teaches men how to deal with our
urges. It's kind of mind-blowing. We can talk about the fruits of
the spirit, how to pray, how to preach, and how to sing praises,
but rarely do we get "real talk" about how to deal with the Dog.
It's taboo to admit that even though you're in the pew and you
love the Lord, even though you're saved, sanctified, and filled
with the Holy Spirit, none of that has stopped you from lusting
after sex, money, and power. This is one of the reasons why there

are fewer men in the church than women: men seek a transparency and honesty that the church doesn't always provide.

There's no doubt the Bible teaches that lust is a sin, yet that's where most ministries stop their teaching. I believe that's where the teaching should begin. We all fall short of the glory of God. We have all sinned. But what we need to know is how to deal with the sin so it doesn't consume our lives. This is why acknowledgment is so critical.

Not admitting to and confronting problems robs us of the ability to solve them. That can lead to explosions of desperate, often destructive, action. Suppressing a feeling is like noticing a leak in your roof but refusing to repair it. Eventually, what was just a few drops that could have been fixed becomes a flood that collapses your roof.

Suppression and Denial

Merriam-Webster defines *suppression* as "the conscious intentional exclusion from consciousness of a thought or feeling." Writing in *Scientific American*, psychotherapist Tori Rodriguez says that acknowledging emotions like fear, regret, and sadness helps us "detoxify the bad experiences" in our lives and support our overall psychological well-being. She goes on to mention; "Suppressing thoughts and feelings can even be harmful." She cites a 2012 Florida State University study in which researchers revealed those "who restrained their thinking more often had stronger stress responses to the cues than did those who suppressed their thoughts less frequently."

When we suppress urges and feelings, they don't go away. They bubble and simmer, and eventually they find an outlet and explode. For example, sexual suppression is the root cause behind the Catholic Church's molestation epidemic. It's the result of centuries of suppressing sexual urges and the emotions behind them.

Men, and women for that matter, simply can't sustain long-term suppression of these urges, especially sexual ones, without healthy outlets (and those healthy outlets don't have to be sex related—more on this later). It's not possible for most anyone to endure long-term emotional suppression in a healthy way, especially men. But some can be tricked into believing they can, because in our society, especially within faith communities, it's not okay for a man to address his weaknesses openly, or to admit that his spiritual commitment isn't enough in and of itself to dismiss the urges.

As a result, men can sometimes believe the spiritual practices of prayer and fasting alone will make the urges disappear, and then can find themselves justifying unacceptable behavior because the urge has gotten so strong that it takes control. Suppressing something doesn't make it go away, it merely gives the object of the suppression greater power.

Suppression and denial go hand in hand. Too often there's a vicious cycle where we suppress urges and then deny that those urges even exist. Medically speaking, *Merriam-Webster* defines *denial* as "a psychological defense mechanism in which confrontation with a personal problem or with reality is avoided by denying the existence of the problem or reality." Does that sound healthy to you? Does that sound like a process in which a strong man confronts and conquers his urges? It doesn't sound like that to me.

For both men and women, have you ever tried to guard against your urges by denying their existence? *I have.* One of the reasons I initially denied the Dog for years was because his lust didn't line up with who I wanted to be or who I professed to be. We put a great deal of pressure on ourselves to present an image that the world will find acceptable, and we hide, suppress, or deny anything that contradicts that image. The last thing in the world I want is to have lustful thoughts or ways. But by denying that they existed in me, I didn't deal with them head on. Roger S. Gil, a mental health clinician who specializes in marriage and family therapy, says this about denial: "Denying reality enables us to continue engaging in an unhealthy behavior . . . most people won't recognize the harmful effects of denial until they are knee-deep in a bad situation. If the same bad outcomes keep happening to us and we can't seem to figure out why, there's a good chance that we are denying reality in some way."

The remedy is for us to face the ugly truth, stop running, and stand and fight for our health, our mental and spiritual well-being!

As I've said, the first solution to this problem is to *feel the urge.* I know this might fly in the face of conventional wisdom, especially from a spiritual perspective. I can just hear the church folk saying, "Boy, what are you talking about 'feel the urge'? You need to cast the urge down!" However, before I can cast anything down, I have to be unafraid to feel that it's there.

Let's talk about fear for a moment. Fear is one of the reasons we suppress these urges in the first place. We're afraid that if we embrace how we're really feeling, we'll lose control. I think the opposite is actually true. Feeling whatever urges and desires we have is the first step to gaining control because I can't change something I don't admit to. We were not given "a spirit of fear" but of power, love, and a sound mind. Don't allow fear to steal the opportunity to learn how to manage this critical area. If you're horny, feel it. If you're hungry, feel it. If you're greedy, feel it.

Feeling Urges Robs Them of Their Power

Once we acknowledge our desires, we allow ourselves to fully feel them, and then we can begin the process of allowing them to pass. That is the goal. I'm not recommending you feel the urges as an excuse to wallow in lust. I'm saying feel the urge but don't act on it.

Now, you are probably thinking I'm crazy, but for the rest of this chapter, I'll share tips and processes for dealing with your urges in a proactive, positive way that gives you strong control over the Dog. Believe it or not, these tips work for women as well as men. I've used these processes many times to manage my urges and get my Dog on a tight leash, and they work. There are many types of urges, but the sexual ones are some of the strongest, so that will be my main focus as we move forward in this chapter.

IN CASE OF FIRE, USE STAIRS

In almost every building in the world there's a sign that says *In case of fire, do not use elevator, use stairs.* This sign provides instruction for how to exit the building safely in the event of a fire. And if we're being honest, when a sexual urge comes upon us, it can feel like a four-alarm fire burning down below. Men need instruction on how to manage those fires (as do women).

The main temptation for the Dog is instant gratification. As Meagan and I wrote about in *The Wait,* the pursuit of instant gratification above all else leads to dangerous, unhealthy choices and prevents you from having the life you want. There is power in delayed gratification. We wrote: "Psychologists, anthropologists, and others have studied self-control and delayed gratification for years. They've found that the ability to say no to immediate, short-term pleasures in favor of lasting ones down the line is linked to better mental and physical health, greater academic success, and more refined social abilities." Our urges are one of the strongest forces that tempt us to practice instant gratification. We feel something, and we want to do something about it, ASAP.

Learning how to manage and effectively deal with urges is essential to personal success. This is the area where men struggle the most and it can lead them to doing all kinds of detrimental things, like cheating, sleeping around, etc., because we haven't spent enough time learning how to handle urges when they arise.

There's no one foolproof method, so try any combination of these ideas that will help you effectively manage these urges. These are tips I've learned as a man dealing with my own urges, yet they can also apply to women having trouble dealing with theirs.

Take a Ten Count

When you feel an urge come on you, the goal is to get it to pass without doing something that would be harmful to yourself, your spirit, your relationship/marriage, or your family. Try counting to ten while breathing deeply. When I underwent conflict resolution training, this was one of the first tricks I learned. Men can be very impulse-driven, so much so that we don't always think before we react.

Instead of stopping and using our reason or deciding on the best course of action, we tend to react out of fear, lust, or the desire for dominance. That reaction can come with ugly consequences. Counting to ten helps reset the mind and let adrenaline dissipate so impulses don't win out. The short pause lets us think. This is a positive step in successfully resolving conflict, and it works the same for lustful urges.

So breathe deeply while counting to ten. You'll calm down and find yourself in a better state to take control instead of letting your urges take control of you. After the ten count, offer up a prayer, and then take a moment to meditate—find your peace. Ask God for the strength not to succumb to the urge. This process has been a tremendous help to me in dealing with unwanted urges and I know it can help you too.

Play Out the Consequences

Another effective tool is to play out in your mind what will likely happen if you follow the desire for instant gratification. When I have done this, the result is a powerful deterrent to acting on an urge, then letting the urge pass and getting on with my day.

For men, suppose you're out and an attractive woman flirts with you. You're flattered, you talk for a bit, and you're already starting to imagine what it would be like to be with her, but there's one big problem: *you are already with someone else*. Stop right there. Play out the sequence of scenes in your head:

1. She invites you back to her place.
2. You go home with her.
3. You have sex.
4. You wake up in the morning and feel terribly guilty about having cheated on your girl.

5. You check your phone: your girl texted you asking if you were okay.

6. Now you have to either own up to what you did and get into a fight (and possibly break up) or start lying, making excuses, and hiding.

7. You lie to your girl.

8. She finds out anyway and she leaves you, and you're heartbroken because you really love her.

9. Her friends, some of whom have become your friends, despise you.

10. Your parents, who love her, can't stand you.

11. Meanwhile, the woman you slept with wants more than a one-night stand.

Stop. Come back to the present. Is everything you just saw in your future worth a single moment of pleasure? If the answer is no—which it should be—then politely bring the conversation to an end and keep moving.

When you project your mind into the future just a little, you'll see that you're risking ruining something really good in your life for a few moments of instant gratification. Remember Newton's Third Law of Motion? *For every action, there is an equal and opposite reaction.* The end result here: unnecessary pain for you, your girl, your families, etc. Doesn't this seem like too high a price to pay? Allowing your mind to play out the consequences can help you avoid doing things you'll ultimately regret.

The same goes for women. If you're engaging with a guy and you know he's in a relationship or married, think about what might happen if you succeed in wooing him. Is it worth the pain and devastation that you would participate in causing? Is it worth causing all that hurt just because you didn't employ the discipline required to manage your urges? Just because you *could* get him doesn't mean you *should* get him. The ends don't justify the means; play out the consequences before you act.

For men who are married, if you are considering stepping out on your wife, I want you to play it out in your mind right now. I want you to see the pain on your wife's face when she finds out you've stepped out. I want you to put yourself in the scene at your house when you come home and she is shattered because she found out that she wasn't the only one. I want you to see the distraught and tearful faces of your children (if you have them) because they discovered Dad has been with someone other than Mom. I want you to see her leaving with the kids because she can't bear the thought of what you've done. Now, I want you to ask yourself: Is any of this worth it? *Play out the consequences mentally before you allow the circumstances to play you.*

Think of Sex as a Want Rather Than a Need

We've all heard Mars Blackmon's famous line "Please, baby, baby, please" from Spike Lee's classic film *She's Gotta Have It*. Is sex a want or a need? I could probably write an entire book on this subject. Whether sex is a want or a need, especially for men, is a question that can get hotly debated. But the answer is irrelevant to the point I want men to consider. To help you accept and get victory over the Dog, consider thinking of sex as something you want, not something you need. I know this might sound completely crazy to you, but follow me for a minute.

I categorize a need as something essential to survival: food, air, shelter, and water. Basically, it's something we will die without. You can joke and say you might not *want* to live without sex (and you just made that joke, didn't you?), but you won't die without it.

A want is something desired but not essential. That's an important distinction, because if something is a need, it's much easier to rationalize what we'll do to get it. So if we put sex on the same level as food, air, shelter, and water, we'll feel justified in doing anything to get it, even if that means manipulating, lying, or cheating.

I wish I had a dollar for every time a woman told me she was dating a man who said to her, "Come on, baby, I need it!"

Men, wanting to have sex is normal, but when you rationalize the pursuit of sex as something that you "just need," you could be consciously or subconsciously preparing yourself to justify any actions to get it. When you see an attractive woman who starts the Dog barking, do you immediately begin telling yourself all the reasons why it would be okay for you to sleep with her or coerce her into sex? If you do, beware. You can start to believe that the ends justify the means—and they *do not*. This is one of the serious dangers of considering sex a need. Suddenly, behavior that you might normally reject as terrible becomes acceptable—*normalized*. If that happens, you've stopped being who you are and can become someone unrecognizable.

However, thinking of sex as a want can help you better manage your urges. Most of us are not accustomed to getting everything we want when we want it, so truth be told, we have a lot of experience living with some of our wants unmet. The same can go for sex. This is why rethinking sex as a want can be more productive in urge management.

Refuse to Rationalize

As I mentioned in the previous chapter, rationalization is a trap. As you are thinking through the consequences of chasing sex, rationalizations may appear in your mind. *Reject them immediately*. Call them out as the lies they are. Here are some common male rationalizations that are never, ever excuses for cheating, one-night stands, harassment, or assault:

- Nobody will ever know.
- You had a hard week.
- Your girlfriend/wife hasn't been in the mood.
- She wanted it.
- She rejected you, so you'll show her.
- Your boys pressured you.
- You and your lady got in a fight.
- You're out of town.
- You're lonely.
- You're alone with her.

- She's a little drunk.
- Just this one time.
- She just invited you back to her place; that doesn't mean you have to have sex.
- She's incredibly hot.
- You just broke up with someone.
- She thinks she's too good for you.

Ever found any of these running through your head as you face a choice between letting the Dog loose and keeping it on its leash? Rationalizations can become moral traps. Let's call them what they are: lies.

Channel Sexual Energy into Creative Energy

One of the most effective ways to get urges under control is to find an alternative outlet for our sexual energy. At its heart, sexual energy (in men and women) is also creative energy. One of the main functions of sex is to create life, but you can redirect that energy to create many different things.

This is a powerful practice if you try it. When you begin to do this, you can become like a real-life Jedi (lol), because the power you will harness to bring about positive change in your life and the world is incredible.

I became celibate in my early twenties, but I didn't get married until my early thirties. Over this period of time, I got really good at channeling my sexual energy into creative energy. During that period, I built a Hollywood career, wrote my first book, spoke around the country, and met Meagan; and I laid down the disciplines and practices that led to my future success. Those years of waiting were incredibly important to my sustainable personal, professional, and creative success. The tangible aspects of my success are a result of channeling my sexual energy into creative energy. *Learn to master your sexual energy and you can master the world.*

In his well-known book *Think and Grow Rich!*, Napoleon Hill devotes an entire chapter to this subject titled "The Mystery of Sex Transmutation." In this powerful chapter he says, "So strong and impelling is the desire for sexual contact that men freely run the risk of life and reputation to indulge it. . . . Fortunate, indeed, is the person who has discovered how to give sex emotion an outlet through some form of creative effort, for he has, by that discovery, lifted himself to the status of a genius."

Give this a try. Turn sexual energy into fuel for your professional life. Next time an urge starts to come upon you, start working on your business plan, finish writing that screenplay, complete that legal brief—do something productive and constructive. Watch what happens. When you transform this energy, your whole world begins to change for the better.

Manage Masturbation

There's an old joke about masturbation: "Ninety-eight percent of people masturbate, and the other two percent are lying about it." I wouldn't be realistic in writing a book like this if I didn't talk about masturbation. It's extremely common with men (and women). Men (and women) turn to masturbation to curb or control their urge for sex, whether they're single or in a relationship.

There are many differing opinions about masturbation. Spiritually, the Bible doesn't mention masturbation at all; ultimately, you have to seek God's will on this for yourself. Practically, however, be careful, because masturbation can lead to the development of unhealthy fantasies that can cause the very act to become addictive. That's why for some it's a slippery slope that could become more destructive than helpful.

We need to get our heads out of the sand when it comes to this topic, especially in communities of faith. The "M word" seems almost as feared as the "F word," and so many curious young boys (and girls) are left to their own devices to figure out where it all fits in the grand scheme of things. This can result in confusion and shame as we cross into manhood and womanhood. Is masturbation bad news? Or an ideal tool for controlling lust?

I love how Napoleon Hill addresses this. He writes, "If it is not transmuted into some creative effort it will find a less worthy outlet." Masturbation is a less worthy outlet for controlling sexual urges. The Dog in a man wants his lower nature to be fed, not the man's higher nature. Masturbation feeds our lower nature, not our higher one. When you masturbate, you drain creative energy that you might otherwise use in a more productive and constructive way.

So before you resort to self-pleasure, ask yourself, "How else could I channel this energy right now?" Find a new hobby, go on an adventure—the possibilities are endless.

Put Down the Porn

Another not-so-secret secret is that for men, masturbation and pornography often go together. Some men call porn a "victimless crime," but I disagree. The victim is men's discipline, his opinion of the value of women, his perception of a healthy sex life, his sex drive, and, if the man becomes addicted to porn, his entire life.

That hasn't stopped the use of pornography from becoming an epidemic. According to a nationwide study conducted by Proven Men Ministries, approximately sixty-four percent of U.S. men admit to viewing porn at least once a month—and Christian men view porn at nearly the same rate. When you break down the results by age, nearly eighty percent of men between the ages of eighteen and thirty view pornography at least monthly, and sixty-seven percent of men between thirty-one and forty-nine do the same.

Wow. The tragedy is that long-term consumption of pornography has been scientifically proven to have plenty of harmful effects. Among other things, it can impair your brain's ability to release the hormones that make you want to have sex with a real partner. It can steer you toward deviant or violent sexual activity, make you less satisfied with real sex, hurt your performance in bed, and become addictive.

The problem is that thanks to the Internet, a monster has been created. According to NBC News, pornography is the *biggest* sector of the entertainment industry, with an estimated net worth of $97 billion. For comparison, all the films released in the U.S. in 2016 earned approximately $11 billion at the box office. If that doesn't blow your mind, try this stat: According to *HuffPost*, porn sites receive more traffic each month than Netflix, Amazon, and Twitter put together.

This is absolutely staggering, because it underscores how powerful the Dog in men is and how much control it has over some men's behavior. Pornography may not be a crime in most cases, but it is definitely not victimless. It hurts those who watch, the partners of those who watch, and those that participate. The Internet has given us what we think is a consequence-free way to let the Dog off its leash, but there are consequences.

I'll never forget the first time I saw a porn film. I was in middle school. Growing up, my brothers, cousins, and I spent a lot of time at our grandparents' house. A friend of the family would always bring my grandfather VHS tapes with multiple movies on them, from *Purple Rain* to *Caddyshack*. So when we would visit my grandparents on the weekend, we would stay up all night watching those movies. It was fun.

One weekend, as we finished the last movie (or so we thought) on the tape, we were horsing around and forgot to hit Stop on the VCR. The next thing you know, a porn movie started playing. We immediately stopped horsing around. We watched with our mouths wide open. At that time, no one in my family had talked to us about the birds and the bees, so seeing this movie was a real eye-opener. Suddenly, these urges rose up in me, the Dog was barking, and it was like we were all in a trance. No matter how hard we tried, we could not turn away until it was over.

Porn is addictive because it stimulates the production of dopamine, the neurotransmitter that triggers pleasure. If you consume porn over and over, your brain stops responding in the same way and you need more and more stimulation to get that dopamine rush. That's how addiction happens. Porn is also addictive because it taps into the deepest, darkest fantasy world in us. Every vile, nasty, profane thought we have can be found somewhere in the world of pornography.

Fight the New Drug is a fantastic website with tremendous resources for anyone struggling with pornography; I highly recommend you check it out. One of the articles on the site talks about Japan's porn problem and how Japanese millennials are remaining virgins not because of chastity but because of porn addiction. This addiction produces a crippling fear of real sex, especially in Japanese men who have become so accustomed to the fantasy world that they are terrified of approaching a woman in the real world. In a post on the site called "How Porn and Technology Are Replacing Sex for Japanese Millennials," they write:

> Let's look at the facts—being hooked on porn can have a huge, negative impact on relationships. As humans, we are designed to have relationships and build connections with others in reality. We *need* the social interaction and sense of community, not the fake intimacy that porn or other technology provide. The more people become hooked on pornography and their virtual "relationships," the more they start missing out on building

those connections. Porn can inhibit viewers from feeling socially able to connect to a potential partner, and shy away from real-life connections altogether, at times. Also, porn has been shown to potentially worsen an anxiety issue, and deepen depression.

There are few statistics on exactly how many men could be considered porn addicts, but considering the number who consume it regularly, I would argue that more men are addicted than we may ever know in our lifetime. And like any addiction, an addiction to porn can gradually make you unrecognizable. Pornography is one of the driving forces that helps turn the Dog into the Beast.

Actor and activist Terry Crews and his amazing wife, Rebecca, are good friends of mine. He shared with me the same revelation he shared with the public a few years ago: pornography almost ruined his life and his marriage. He said pornography "really, really messed up my life." He then went on Facebook in a series of video posts to reveal how badly it messed him up:

Some people say, "Hey, man . . . you can't really be addicted to pornography." But I'm gonna tell you something: If day turns into night and you are still watching, you probably have got a problem. And that was me.

It changes the way you think about people. People become objects. People become body parts; they become things to be used rather than people to be loved.

It affected everything. My wife was literally like, "I don't know you anymore. I'm out of here." I had to change. I literally had to go to rehab for it.

Every time I watched it, I was walled off. It was like another brick that came between me and my wife. And the truth is, everything you need for intimacy is in your (partner).

CNN reported that there were thousands of comments left on Terry's Facebook page thanking him for his transparency:

Thank you so much for this message, Terry. Your honesty humbles me. I don't smoke, I don't drink, I don't do drugs. But I have wrestled for years—YEARS—with pornography. I am grateful today to say that I have a very specific sobriety date and I have stayed clean for some time now. I work at it every day and I do everything I can to remove its power and hold.

"Thanks for putting this out there and congratulations on finding recovery," said a female commenter. "This horrible plague killed my marriage. Glad you decided to fight. We need more voices bringing awareness. There is a silent war being fought and the casualties are families and relationships."

I applaud Terry for his courage in sharing what few men would dare admit. Meanwhile, those comments on Facebook are both powerful and revealing. Men are struggling with this. It's ruining men. *Pornography feeds the Dog; it will NOT help you manage it.* It doesn't quell lust; it grows it. It will turn you into someone you don't want to be. If you don't watch it, don't start.

If you do, stop. Delete the apps and bookmarks and invest in one of the many porn blocking software applications you can put on your computer. For more help, visit Fightthenewdrug .org. They have many great resources.

Lastly, my close friend, Grammy Award–winning recording artist Kirk Franklin, went public years ago about his addiction to pornography. He told me one of the keys to breaking his addiction was the idea "as a man thinketh"—he didn't want to turn into the lustful thoughts that pornography made him think about. That one idea helped him break free from its destructive grip. He also believes that overcoming the addiction is as much spiritual as it is practical. Similar to a 12-step program, coming out of a porn addiction will require a spiritual commitment. On your own you may not have the strength, yet the power of God working in you combined with these practical tips can help you overcome.

Of course, men are not the only ones who struggle with porn addiction. Plenty of women have the very same temptations, and it's not any easier for them to break free. Ladies, if you struggle with watching porn, I encourage you to stop and refocus your energy on the real relationships in your life. And if you're in a relationship with a man who struggles with porn? Terry Crews says, "Women, you need to be fearless. You need to confront your man about this problem. You cannot accept any pornography in your life."

I'm not usually one to encourage invasion of privacy, but when it's a choice between your man's privacy and his well-being, I believe his well-being (and yours, for that matter) is more important. Pornography is toxic, so if you suspect your man has a problem with consuming porn, you should investigate. If you suspect that he has a porn habit, talk to him about it. I know this isn't easy, but if he loves you he will want to get help, and while he may be angry at first, he will ultimately thank you.

Get Your Workout On

Exercise and fitness are also excellent ways to manage urges. There have been many studies with differing conclusions about whether working out diminishes or enhances our sex drive, but what I know from experience is that working out is an excellent way to redirect sexual energy into something productive. Devoting more time to working out, exercising, or playing a sport will help you lose weight, be healthier, have more energy, look better, and do more of what you care about.

Curb Your Appetite

The practice of celibacy while I was single took me to another level. As I've mentioned, it contributed to much of my success. In *The Wait*, Meagan and I made our position very clear: the ideal situation is to wait until marriage to have sex. I believed then and still believe that is the optimal design for us as human beings in terms of harmony and mitigating damage to the spirit.

Meagan and I meet many amazing women who are doing the Wait yet have trouble finding men who will wait with them. I can tell you this: making the commitment to stop having sex until marriage will change everything for the better in a man's life. While Meagan and I were on vacation in Jamaica, I ran into a guy who told me that based on our book, he started doing the Wait, and it took his life to a different level. Because he learned impulse control, he had more time to think and build his business into a success. Waiting will help you manage your urges and so much more!

However, no matter what I say, I know that some of you may not be willing to make that choice. So I will say this: If you don't choose to wait until marriage, I highly recommend that you only have sex in the context of a monogamous, loving relationship. Sex outside that kind of relationship is what I call "Dog food." But there's another good reason to show restraint, even if you are in a relationship. No matter how much you want to love your partner, you can't help but reference your sexual experiences before you came together. You will think about whom you've been with and whom they've been with. This can become a source of conflict and unhappiness because your partner may never be able to live up to the level of the previous sexual encounters you've experienced.

If you choose not to wait until marriage, then monogamy, commitment, and honesty are the best path. Chasing endless, meaningless sexual experiences and letting your urges run wild will sabotage your future relationships—and your current one.

DEALING WITH NONSEXUAL URGES

Many of the tips I've laid out for dealing with sexual urges can also help you manage nonsexual ones. For example, you can apply "playing out the consequences" to greed or a lustful desire for career advancement. Before you decide to go behind your colleague's back, present an idea that is someone else's as your own, or cheat to get ahead, play out the consequences. Picture what will happen when you get caught, fired, and even worse, your entire professional reputation is ruined. Then ask yourself, is it worth it? Here are two other important ways to manage nonsexual urges.

Unplug from Social Media

Social media is one of the main initiators of greed, covetousness, and envy. While it's a lot of fun to share pictures or stories on Instagram, Facebook, Twitter, or Snapchat, there's also a serious downside to social media. As we scroll through other pages, it's very easy for our urges for advancement, money, and power to be incited. We see others having what we want and we begin to ask, "Why hasn't this happened for me yet?" I can't even begin to tell you how many people have told me how many hours they spend on social media a day. Don't get caught in the social media trap. Manage it so it doesn't manage you. If you feel these unhealthy urges rise up in you, limit the amount of time you devote to being on social media each day. There have been periods where I have to disengage from social media completely because of the negative feelings it can sometimes produce within me. During these times of unplugging, I've been able to get my peace back, and I highly recommend you try it.

Practice Patience

Most of us struggle with impatience in some area of our life. "When am I getting promoted?" "When can I afford a new house?" "Why did I get overlooked?" "When is my time?" These types of questions can produce an urge within us that makes us impatient. Impatience can lead to depression, anxiety, and discontent. It can also lead us to rush the process of personal and professional development, which can lead to setbacks. Everything you want in life will require time to achieve. Be persistent in working toward your goals, yet practice patience every day. As long as you stay committed to the process of success you will achieve all that you desire and more no matter how long it takes.

THE ACCEPTANCE PRAYER FOR MEN

Dear God,

Help me right now deal with the pain and guilt I feel over the things I've done. I've done things I'm not proud of, things that make me feel guilty and ashamed. So ashamed I don't even feel worthy of this prayer and of the calling of my life. I'm sorry for the pain I've caused so many women in my life. Please heal any woman I've hurt. I'm sorry for all the hearts I've recklessly broken. I'm sorry for the way I've acted even when I knew better. I feel so broken at times, I feel hopeless. I need your help, God, show me the way! Forgive me for my wrongdoings and give me the courage to right all the wrongs I've committed. I desperately want to do better, I need to do better, help me do better! I can't keep living like this, I've got to break free and become a man of my word! I need healing and I need to help heal any situation or circumstance I've messed up. Give me the strength to be the man I was created to be and give me the power to walk in it daily. I will become the man of destiny I was created to be!

In the mighty name of Jesus,

Amen

THE ACCEPTANCE PRAYER FOR WOMEN

Dear Lord,

I accept that there are things I have had to endure that I may never understand. I ask you for healing emotionally, mentally, physically, and spiritually. Please give me comfort in the times when discomfort is the only feeling available to me. I accept that you have created me for greatness and I commit myself to pursuing it each and every day. I accept that there are some men who cannot handle all you have created me to be, but I will not make myself smaller to fit into their limited view of who I am! I no longer accept any man who can't respect me! I no longer accept anyone who tries to make me feel inferior! I no longer accept feelings of insecurity or lack of self-worth! I accept the fullness of my calling and destiny! I accept the power of the woman you have created me to be! I will not live quietly; I roar with the excellence and authority you have given me from this day forward!

In the mighty name of Jesus,

Amen

CHAPTER 3

MASTER THE DOG

Sho'nuff: "All right, Leroy. Who's the one and only Master?"

Leroy Green: "I am."

—BERRY GORDY'S *THE LAST DRAGON*

You will never have a greater or lesser dominion than that over

yourself . . . He who cannot establish dominion over himself

will have no dominion over others.

—LEONARDO DA VINCI

By nature, dogs understand a specific social structure, and that structure is based on leadership. In the wild, every pack of dogs has a leader, an "alpha dog." Even when they've been domesticated, dogs still look for this leadership. A dog will look for a master. If you own a dog and you don't lead the dog, the dog will lead you. It won't listen when you give a command. It will pursue its own pleasures instead of what you want it to do. It will do whatever it wants, and neither of you will end up happy about it.

That's because every dog needs a master who can provide guidance, training, and leadership. Being a master isn't just declaring yourself in charge; it's about earning a dog's respect so that it will listen to you. Believe it or not, dogs are more willing to please masters who command respect.

To gain a dog's respect, you have to teach it what is expected and be consistent in expecting it; these are essential for gaining respect and obedience. In "Fifteen Steps to Becoming the Pack Leader," renowned dog trainer Graham Bloem says, "It is the combined effort of learned behaviors and sound leadership that will create lasting results and a great relationship of love and mutual respect."

In other words, there's a distinct difference between being a dog owner and a dog master. An owner wants respect, and often doesn't get it. A master earns it. A master earns that respect through love. When a dog owner loves their dog enough to discipline it, then that is when true respect is achieved.

This same idea is at work in every man. Every man has a Dog and a Master within. As I've mentioned, the Dog represents lust, yet the Master represents the love in men. Just as a master commands and controls a real dog through discipline, confidence, and love, the Master in men has the power to control the Dog by the same means. However, just because there is a Master in men, that doesn't automatically make a man a Master. Think of the difference between being a male and being a man. Anatomically there are billions of males on the planet, yet not every male takes on the responsibility of manhood. There are plenty of males who are trapped in boyhood. What's the difference between a boy and a man? The same difference between a dog and its master: leadership.

Being a man requires becoming a leader on a personal level. Just because a man is a great leader professionally doesn't make him a great leader personally. There have been many books written about male leadership and how to succeed profession- ally, yet I believe true success starts within and begins with commitment, communication, determination, and courage. In our society, we overemphasize external success, and many of us have fallen into the trap of thinking that's all that matters. This thinking has led many men and women into massive failure. Focusing on external development at the expense of internal development is a recipe for disaster. This is one of the reasons I encourage both men and women to not evaluate men solely by their professional accomplishments but by their personal integ- rity. That's the real barometer of true success.

There are many ways a man can tap into his inner Master, but it all starts with taking personal leadership. A dog owner who wants to become a master has to learn to take leadership of their dog by projecting confidence, establishing authority, teaching commands, and asserting control. In the same way, any man who aspires to Mastery must also do the same within himself.

WHO'S THE MASTER?

Have you ever been to the park and seen a dog running wild on a leash while the owner struggles to get it to calm down? I've seen this many times, but I recently learned that this is a sign that the dog is in control, not its master. Also, if you go for a walk and the dog insists on walking ahead of you instead of beside you, this is also a sign that the dog is in control. Just because you're holding the leash doesn't mean you're the one in control.

As I grew into adulthood, I became even more aware of the battle for control within me. As I felt the Dog rising up, I felt a force of love, the Master, rising up in me that was equally strong, if not more so. Love is the most powerful force in the universe and this is why when we work on putting it in control, it can help us succeed at mastering lust. The Master is love; it is the truest, deepest desire in men to be good, honorable, and noble. The Master is man as God intended him to be. The Master is the highest part of a man—the part that loves himself, loves his family, loves remaining committed to his relationship, loves honesty, loves acting with integrity, loves thriving on discipline. It's also the part of the man that is powerful, charismatic, and assertive while being compassionate and vulnerable. I realized that when I focused on following what the Master in me was compelling me to do, I felt peace. But sometimes it was hard to hear his voice.

One of the reasons is because as men we aren't taught how to love. We're taught how to make money, get women, buy a house, lease a car, and achieve the promotion, but we are rarely taught how to love, especially how to love ourselves. We understand love as a concept, yet most men I know struggle with putting it into practice consistently. I know I've struggled with it mostly because I've had a hard time truly loving myself. Growing up I always felt like I didn't fit in (for most I was too square) and as a result, I didn't really like who I was. As I came into adulthood I began to realize that everything good I wanted in life was tied up in love, but first I had to learn to love myself. I've found it's hard to know how to love others when you don't know how to love yourself. Let's define *love*. *Merriam-Webster* defines it like this:

love

noun | ləv

1   a (1) : strong affection for another arising out of kinship or personal ties

(2) : attraction based on sexual desire : affection and tenderness felt by lovers

2   warm attachment, enthusiasm, or devotion . . .

3   a : unselfish loyal and benevolent

see benevolent 1a) concern for the good of another: such as

(1) : the fatherly concern of God for humankind

(2) : brotherly concern for others

Over the years, as I've nurtured the Master within by learning to love and accept who I am, flaws and all, I've come to discover many things about Masters I want to share with you. Masters are stronger than any Jedi, and more capable of bringing about positive change in the world than anyone carrying a lightsaber.

Many men allow the Dog within to control them because they don't understand the idea of the Master. Here are the basics of what men and women need to know about Masters.

Masters Are More Powerful Than Dogs

Masters are not passive or soft. Masters are ambitious and confident without being arrogant or intimidating. The Dog is always testing and trying to get off its leash. It never takes a vacation. The man who wants to be a Master must accept the fact that while some days might be easier than others, there are no days off. Because of this, it's easy to wind up feeling powerless against the Dog. But while the Dog is strong, the Master can bring him to heel.

How? Because the Dog seeks material and sexual validation, but Masters know they are already validated. The Dog wants men to believe that validation comes from what they own, how much money or power they have, and who's in their bed. But the Master knows that's a lie. That is the false sense of manhood. It's an illusion. When external pursuits are used as the basis of a man's self-worth, then that man will always be in search of validation, because anything external can be taken away. Masters seek validation from within. The bedrocks of personal validation are integrity, character, constancy, faithfulness, kindness, and courage.

For men, the Master is who you are. It can never be taken from you. I want you to get this deep in your spirit: The mere fact of your birth validates you. There is nothing illegitimate about you. You were created to be great and fulfill your calling and destiny. When you truly believe this, you will allow yourself to experience a new dimension of confidence, power, and peace.

Women, you might be in a tough spot with the man you love if he's been acting more like the Dog than the Master. I need you to know there is hope, because there is a Master in him that has way more power than the Dog. He just might need your assistance in calling the Master out of him and giving him the confidence to step forward. Telling the man in your life that he is worthy, that he is valued, and that he is loved for exactly who he is at his core—saying it over and over until he starts to believe it—could help him find the courage to bring the Master forward.

Masters Take Control

Kirk Cushing of The Dog Masters says, "Sometimes, your dog will need tough love. This is not to be confused with rough love. Tough love is when you put the baby voice away, enforce your authoritative role, and set your boundaries." Masters aren't afraid to take control and exert aggressive force over the Dog.

Remember, the Dog doesn't want to be disciplined. It'll resist. It's like a spoiled child; it doesn't cooperate. It knows there are no real consequences for doing what it wants instead of what you ask of it. And, like a spoiled child, it will push the limits to see just how much it can get away with.

If a man wants to get control over it, half measures won't work. Men, in order to train the Dog, you have to be the alpha male—you have to be aggressive, stand firm, and take control. The first step is deciding that you don't want to let the Dog win any longer. When you get tired and fed up with living beneath your calling because deep down you know there is a better way to live, make the decision that you want the Master to be in control, and then stop ignoring the Dog. Let the love in you rise up over the lust in you. Decide to set boundaries and use tough love to exert self-control.

Women, if you feel the Dog in your man has been in control more than the Master, you can demand that the Master in your man take control. I don't mean take control as a form of domination over you—I mean appealing to the love in your man to rise up and take control of his life. A great preacher once said that there's a king and a fool in every man. Whenever he'd act badly, his wife wouldn't ignore the fool in him, but she spoke to the king in him, and that motivated him to put away his foolish behavior and put the king within in charge of his life. Don't ignore your man's behavior, but try to appeal to the love in him that wants to be the man God created him to be. When you do this, you affirm the love and help it grow. Most men will never tell you this but they are in need of your positive affirmations more than you may ever know.

Masters Know the Commands

There are five basic commands that most dog trainers say every dog should know: "Come," "Stay," "Sit," "Heel," and "Down." In his book *Dog Training*, Michael Kenssington says, "Most obedience programs consider a dog well-trained when they are able to follow each of these commands every time they are given."

You're going to laugh at me, but I don't care. I will share my truth if it will help set someone free. Sometimes, when the Dog starts to rise in me, I will yell commands at myself: "Sit!" or "Stop!" or "No!" I know it's a funny thought, but it helps. I must let the Dog know I'm in charge at all times. He is under my authority and not the other way around. There is no room for compromise, because either the Master or the Dog will be in control in a given moment. If the Dog has control, the Master will succumb to its power. If the Master has control, then the Dog will bend to his will. Men, use whatever healthy tools you must to control the Dog, including talking to yourself.

Women, you can use these commands too. If you're in a dating situation and the man is moving too fast, just whip out a "Heel" on him. In dog training, *heel* means the dog is required to keep pace with the owner, stopping when the owner stops and walking when the owner walks. Sometimes that Dog wants to get ahead of you and you've got to let it know you aren't having that.

Masters Are Committed to Becoming Better

You're probably familiar with the proverb "The road to hell is paved with good intentions." Good intent is important, but becoming the Master is about turning intention into action. Actions matter. Actions are how we make an impact on the world and care for the people in our lives. When men allow their actions to come from the love inside (and not from the lust within), those actions can have a positive and life-changing impact on themselves and those around them, especially the women in their life.

Men, while you might do important things in life and have great ambitions, it's critical to never lose sight of who you are working to become. Why? Because that determines every bit of success, happiness, and peace you will ever enjoy.

I used the phrase *working to become* deliberately. Becoming the Master isn't about hitting perfection and then being satisfied. Masters are always working to be their best self and serve their highest purpose. Men aren't at their best when they're comfortable and complacent. Men are at their best when they're striving toward a goal, especially when that goal is becoming the best man they can be—a goal that demands discipline and hard work.

That's certainly true for me. I'm on the hunt every day to become my true self. I ask myself these two questions constantly: Who was I created to be? and What problem in the world was I created to solve?

These questions keep the Master in me hungry to discover the answers. I encourage both men and women to ask themselves these questions regularly. But I will offer a word of caution. It's easy to get depressed when the answers aren't readily apparent. Don't allow depression to set in. These are some of life's biggest questions, and it will take time, commitment, and patience for these answers to be revealed. That doesn't mean you should stop asking and striving to figure out the answers, though. The search for the answers will inspire you to reach for the Master in you.

Masters Manage Desires

As I've mentioned, dogs desire pleasure. And if an owner constantly gives in to a dog's desires, it will limit the owner's ability to discipline the dog when needed. A dog owner must become the manager of the dog's desires in order to train the dog properly.

The desires of the Dog never go away, no matter how religious or respected a man might be. Our desires, good or bad, have power over our daily behavior and desire management is the key to life management.

The quality of your life depends on the desires you choose to pursue and those you choose to forgo.

Masters learn how to manage their desires. Every day we all have to choose between fulfilling desires that are appropriate (good) and desires that are inappropriate (bad). Masters choose to fulfill the desires that enhance well-being and avoid those that don't.

For women, be mindful of the desires you help the man in your life manage. You can play a positive and negative role in this area. Helping and affirming the Master within is what positive desire management looks like. However, I've seen some women become codependent, feeding the desires of the Dog instead of the Master. This is what negative desire management looks like. Codependency can mean you become a crutch instead of a healthy support system. What's the difference between helping in a positive way and becoming codependent? Responsibility. No matter how much you want to help build up the Master in the man you're with, don't do his work for him. A man can only become a Master by taking full responsibility for his life and his choices (both personal and professional). You can help him achieve his goals, but be careful not to fall into the trap where you are the one doing so much of his work that he doesn't bear the brunt of the responsibility for the fulfillment of his own goals.

Masters Channel Energy Positively

Beware of the Dog's energy. It's primal and compelling and more powerful than the Force. The energy that comes from the Dog feels raw, fun, and carefree, but don't be fooled—it's not innocent. The energy of lust has to be channeled into something positive to prevent its destructive grip from taking hold. It's like electricity: it has the potential to be lethal, but when it's properly channeled, it can light your way.

Remember what I said about channeling sexual energy into creative energy? Masters channel the Dog's energy to use as a resource because they've decided that lust will not get the best of them. That can be a real advantage, because the Dog's energy is the same as that male passion, desire, and ambition for exploration and risk. I practice channeling this energy into my marriage, my workouts, my writing, my producing, and even my preaching. For example, when a lustful feeling arises about another woman, I channel that energy into a thought about my wife: *I can't wait until I see her.* It's powerful stuff. The Master has the power to transform the Dog's energy into a force to be used for good.

Masters Commit

Don't be impressed by a man's toys (houses, cars, money, even fame). The sign of what a man truly values can be found in his commitments. Evaluate every man with this question: What is he committed to? His commitments—or lack thereof—will reveal if the Master or the Dog is in control, especially when it comes to women.

Women ask me all the time, "Why are men afraid to commit to one woman?" There are many answers to this question. Sometimes men don't want to commit because they are uncertain if the woman they are dating is the right one.

However, some men intentionally avoid commitment because they are addicted to the chase. For example, even though I was celibate for years before getting married, that doesn't mean I was always the best dater. There were times when the Dog was in control and I was addicted to the practice of going from one woman to the next. I loved to date carelessly and selfishly until I realized the damage I was inflicting on myself and on the women I was with. Picture a kid in a candy store who eats as much candy as they can possibly stand. It feels great while it's happening, but when the sugar rush is over, what's left behind is an achy stomach and rotten teeth.

There are so many men who consistently run from commitment yet still want to have their fill of women. They don't always realize the long-term damage (physical, emotional, and spiritual) they are doing to themselves and to the women they are dealing with. Consistently dating multiple women can build an unhealthy appetite, and eventually committing to just one doesn't suffice.

There are other men who are terrified of commitment because they got their heart broken in the past. Now they date around as a way to protect themselves from ever being vulnerable so their heart can't be broken again. Women, men may want to pretend like they don't have feelings, but please don't believe the hype. There are many men who are still reeling from a devastating heartbreak, and that affects the way they interact with women now. Men are more sensitive than you might realize.

There are some men who don't commit because they never saw commitment modeled in the home they grew up in. Maybe they come from a home where their mother and father weren't together, or if they were together, they argued all the time. There are some men who grew up with the only male figures in their lives being men who had multiple women; as a result, they have modeled this behavior. Also, there are some men who had negative relationships with their mothers, and this impacts how they view women and themselves. The relationships a man had with his mother and father growing up have a significant impact on their desire or unwillingness to commit to one relationship as an adult. This was very true in my life.

As I mentioned earlier, my father died when I was nine. My mother did an outstanding job of raising my brothers and me in his absence; however, my mom and I didn't always have the best relationship when I was growing up. Her mother (my grandmother) had my great-grandmother raise my mother until she was about twelve years old. My mother felt abandoned by my grandmother, which caused my mother to struggle with accepting that she was really loved. So, she loved my brothers and me the best she knew how, yet from my vantage point as a kid it wasn't enough. There were times when we would argue and I would tell her that she didn't love me and this would cut her to the core and she would say, "I've done more for you than was done for me. At least I never gave you up, I kept you." Even now as I write these words, I tear up. Growing up I wasn't always aware of the deep pain she carried and I didn't become aware of the magnitude of what she was saying until I got much older. Now our relationship is amazing and as I've matured, I've come to understand the power of her love and sacrifice. The absence of my father and the relationship I had with my mother directly impacted my dating life. As I got older and started dating, I had tremendous difficulty committing. The longest relationship I ever had before I got married was two years. It wasn't until meeting Meagan that I really faced my fear of commitment, and it hasn't been easy, but it has been healing and deeply rewarding.

Whatever the reason, I challenge any man reading this to face your fear of commitment head-on. Stop running from it. When you commit to the right woman, your life increases, not decreases. Dating without an eye toward commitment takes away valuable time and energy from your purpose, not to mention the pain you can cause to so many women. Having multiple women just for the sake of having multiple women is child's play, and I challenge you to stop playing, put away your toys, and do the grown man business of committing. There's a Master in you that thrives off commitment.

Go back to the story of Adam and Eve in Eden. God said, "It is not good that the man should be alone." That statement was the impetus behind God's creation of Eve from the rib of Adam. Adam was the one who said, "This is now bone of my bones, and flesh of my flesh," then the text says, "Therefore shall a man leave his father and his mother, and shall cleave unto his wife: and they shall be one flesh" (Genesis 2:23–24). From the very beginning, men were created with a need for women, not vice versa. There is actually no mention of Eve having the same need for Adam. This is important because in my experience, so many men run from committing to a woman, yet the story of Adam and Eve demonstrates that men need women. It's part of our makeup. Men, committing to the right woman can provide the fulfillment you've been longing for.

Women, be careful of the man who is perpetually un-committed. If he has no commitments in his life—to other people, his family, his work, to the church, or something in his life other than himself—steer clear. Don't just assume you can change him—if you are dating a man or about to date one, ask him about his philosophy on commitment and if it's something he's struggled with in the past. It may feel uncomfortable, but you need to know what you're getting yourself into. I know many women will hesitate to ask a question like this, because they're afraid it will scare the man away, thinking he'll assume she's asking for a ring on the spot. Don't be afraid. As long as you ask the question gently, earnestly, and openly, without demanding any kind of commitment in that moment, a Master will answer honestly. And don't necessarily be afraid to move forward if he admits that commitment is something he has struggled with in the past. If he answers honestly, it's a good sign. You'll be going into a relationship with your eyes open.

MASTERS PRACTICE MASTERY

Continue obedience training throughout his life.
It should be a part of a daily routine.
–GRAHAM BLOEM

Men, as difficult as it is, we have to do our work. No matter how many lustful thoughts we may have, we have to get to the place where we decide we aren't going to act on them. Where we aren't going to backstab our way to the top or go into debt trying to present an image we think will impress others while we privately suffer. We have to refuse to allow those thoughts to become things that destroy us. Transparency is the key to transformation. So we've got to be open, honest, and committed.

(Women, hold on, I've got to speak to the men for a moment. If we, as men, can tap into the Master within us, I believe this will help solve the problems that both men and women have. I'll come back to you in a little while.)

If you're a man who has been suffering at the hands of the Dog, how do you change? How do you get back in control of your lust and become a better man? The Master has the power to assert authority over the Dog. The only sure way to control it is Mastery. Masters practice Mastery.

Mastery is a man's lifelong process of becoming his highest and best self. As with anything, it takes repetition, dedication, and patience. It requires practice—twenty-four hours a day, 365 days a year. Mastery is the work of a lifetime, like fitness, golf, or music. Every great golfer is always in pursuit of the perfect swing, knowing it will take a lifetime to master the game. Fitness is the work of a lifetime, because true health means transforming who you are cell by cell. Becoming a great musician means becoming your instrument—*becoming your music*. That's what Mastery is—a lifetime commitment.

Mastery is the highest form of success. Mastery is the key to peace (and peace is the ultimate hallmark of success) because it helps reduce the chaos that living doggishly creates. Being a Dog is expensive financially, emotionally, and spiritually.

When we choose a better life, we become worthy of the life
we choose.

Men, you can master the Dog and keep your life free of self-generated stress, drama, and pain. Inside you right now, you're already the man who wants to commit to the right woman (a woman as worthy of you as you are of her), a man who isn't fueled by greed and self-preservation. Inside you is a man who is truly committed to being and contributing to the greater good. You can get control over the Dog! It's just like starting a workout program. You have to find a routine and incorporate it into your life, while at the same time clearing out everything that stands in the way of your goal. Clear out the apps, links, phone numbers, and social media followers that aren't good. Block the numbers of men and women who are toxic. Go cold turkey on clubs or other places that are danger zones. Make it harder for the Dog to get excited and it will be easier to feel like a Master.

Mastery = Peace. Success = Peace. Mastery = Success.

Now, I've spent plenty of time getting philosophical or waxing poetic about the power and necessity of Mastery. But practically, what does it look like? Mastery can take many forms. Here's what it looks like in some of the main areas that affect our lives.

MASTERY IN DATING

We're living in the boom of a hookup culture. Never before in the history of human society has it been easier to hook up with no strings attached. The advances in technology and the popularity of apps have proven to be a lucrative yet toxic combination. Apps like Casualx and Tinder allow you to swipe until your heart is content or until you find the right person who is also looking for a casual hang. According to Mashable, Tinder boasts 1.6 billion swipes a day! While turning dating into a game of swipes might be fun, I believe it's doing untold damage to both men and women. How? When the sole focus of dating becomes self-centered physical satisfaction with little to no emotional regard for the person from which the satisfaction is being derived, it creates this "me first" mentality. This works against the construction of genuine connection and companionship, which is the foundation of healthy dating.

The health and well-being of our society is directly linked to how we date. If we date better, then we marry better. If we marry better, then we parent better. If we parent better, then we "family" better. And a healthy family is the foundation of a healthy society.

Here are some of the dangerous myths about men that work against healthy dating:

- *Real men sleep with as many women as possible.*
- *Real men don't commit.*
- *Real men don't show their feelings.*

The opposite of each is true. Real men don't dominate, intimidate, or coerce women into becoming their sexual playthings. Real men regard women as people, not objects of sexual gratification. They understand that women may want to be seen as sexy, but that doesn't mean they want to be treated as a sex object. He wants a woman not for what she can do sexually but for who she is mentally, spiritually, and emotionally. Real men honor commitments and act with fidelity. Real men reveal their feelings, including weaknesses, doubts, and fears. If a man aspires to Mastery, it must show up in his dating life.

Be Honest with Women About Your Intentions

When a man goes out on a date, he should be clear and direct about what he expects. He shouldn't create false expectations to get companionship and/or sex from a woman. If a man isn't interested in a committed relationship, then he should tell her the truth. He shouldn't lie to her and then step out on her later. Here are some questions to ask when you're thinking about Mastery in dating.

For men:

- How many hearts have you broken because you didn't have control of the Dog?
- How many times have you been in a long-term relationship with a woman but have never been able to commit to more?
- How often have you thought a woman was the one until you got to know her better and realized she was human and had flaws, just like everyone else?
- How many women have you misled to get sex and then lost interest in them?

- How many women are you dating right now who think they're the only one?

For women:

- How many times has a man you thought you could trust lied to you?
- How many times have you excused or overlooked a man's behavior, assuming you could make him change?
- How many times have you had sex with a man and found out after the fact that that was all he wanted?
- Have you ever believed you had to accept a man's flaws or behavior, thinking he might be the best you could get or that you've already invested too much in the relationship to walk away now?
- How many times have you been rejected by a man because he wouldn't honor your standards?

To become a Master in dating, there must be transparency and honesty. So single men, let's get real. If you're playing around or cheating on someone or being flat-out disrespectful right now as you read this, these questions are for you:

If someone were doing to your sister what you're doing to the women in your dating life, would you allow it?

If your answer is no, then why would you treat someone else's sister in a manner that is unacceptable to you?

If a man was dogging out your mother or your daughter by lying to her and sleeping around on her, what would you do if you had a chance to look that man in the face?

If your answer involves wanting to lay hands on that man, then look at yourself. Why is it okay for you to do the same things to someone else's mother or daughter?

The man who keeps secrets and lies about his intentions is the Dog, not the Master. Just be honest if you are in a period of your life where you're not seriously looking. It's okay—just be truthful with whomever you're dating. If you don't value and respect her, don't date her.

Ladies, as I've mentioned before, getting clear on a man's intentions can help you stay out of the gray area. There are a couple of things to be mindful of when assessing a man's intentions. When he tells you he doesn't want to be in a relationship, believe him. I've seen many women disregard what a man says because his actions seem to be saying otherwise. If a man says he doesn't want to be in a relationship, then don't allow yourself to get in a situation where you are falling into relationship behavior with him (spending every day together, meeting your family and friends, etc.). Don't let him have those benefits without the commitment.

However, if he tells you his intentions for you are good, don't just take him at his word. Remember the Dog is a master manipulator. Evaluate his actions to see if they back up his talk, and if they don't, beware.

The Master Wants a Woman, the Dog Just Wants a . . .

When a male dog is in heat, he looks for a female dog that can help him get satisfaction. Then he moves on. The Dog in a man acts the same way. When a man gets horny, he'll be on the lookout for a way to resolve that feeling. There will always be some women who are willing to accommodate him on this.

Men, be mindful of a woman who feeds your Dog with no strings attached. There are *always* strings attached, and not all women have pure intentions. There are some women who seek to manipulate and exploit you because they know that lust is your weakness. There have been many men who lost everything because they allowed themselves to be manipulated by a woman who played upon their lust intentionally. This is why it's so important to build up the Master in you, so you have the strength to say no. Just because it's offered doesn't mean you have to take it.

Women, every situation is different, so there are exceptions to this rule. However, in my experience, I've learned that a woman has to be careful how she goes about getting a man. If you appealed to the Dog to get the man then once you have him you want the Master to show up, you're fooling yourself. Be aware: you can't date the Dog and marry the Master.

As many of you have already experienced, it's easy to appeal to a man's lust. But what are the long-term repercussions of doing this? You can potentially be viewed as only an object of his lust, and if you want something more significant from him, it may never materialize. You have the power to choose what you want and to make choices in dating that will help you achieve it. Yes, it will require sacrifice because many men aren't leading with the Master (hopefully this book will change that) so some men will reject you if you don't immediately appeal to their lustful desires. That's okay—rejection is God's protection. Protect your heart, mind, body, and soul until you come across the right man who's willing to love and be loved.

Great Women Are Attracted to Masters

Women of character and substance are attracted to Masters because Masters are visionaries. They are purposeful, and committed to being and doing well. They're good partners, lovers, and parents. They're charismatic and confident, which makes them attractive. There's no way in the world an amazing woman like Meagan would have been attracted to me if I hadn't already been practicing Mastery when we met. Don't believe the hype: being a Dog only takes a man so far. Being a Master is everything!

Men, if you want to attract the woman of your dreams, be kind, considerate, and passionate about your purpose. Many women have told me how attractive it is to see a guy who's on a positive mission in life.

MASTERY IN MARRIAGE

A strong marriage requires two people who choose to love each
other even on those days when it's a struggle to like each other.

—DAVE WILLIS, COFOUNDER OF STRONGERMARRIAGES.COM

Marriage is the area where men and women can have some of
the most intense struggles. Truth be told, no one can tell you
how to be married until you actually are married. You think
you have an idea of what it is, but then you realize you had no
idea what it would be like until you are married. This becomes
an area of deep struggle for many, because there isn't a manual
on how to be a husband or a wife, how to care properly for
your spouse, or how to rediscover who you are now that you're
a unit. With that being said, if a man aspires to Mastery, marriage is the perfect training ground to achieve it. Here's what
Mastery in marriage looks like. I could write an entire book on
this subject alone, but for now I'll give you a couple of the most
pressing issues the Master has to deal with.

Don't Be Afraid to Communicate Openly About Sexual Needs

I'm starting with this one because this is an area where so many
marriages suffer. The infrequency of sex in marriage can become a major point of contention and can cause both men and
women to become deeply frustrated to the point of helplessness.
Beware of the Dog, because this is when it speaks the loudest

and men can find themselves vulnerable to stepping out on their wife or finding unhealthy outlets to fill the void.

Men, if you aren't having sex frequently enough with your wife, don't be afraid of communicating openly with her about your needs. However, know this: if you're feeling this way, she's probably feeling this way too. The Master must create a safe, nonjudgmental environment in order to have the conversation. You might even want to write down how you feel, your frustrations regarding your sex life, and your honest desire to find a solution so when you talk with her you can stay focused and calm. There have been times when Meagan and I have discussed this issue and I was upset and didn't handle the conversation well. As a result, she completely shut down. However, after handling it so poorly, I regrouped and when I was more loving, understanding, and sensitive, I brought it up again, and that change in attitude helped us find common ground so we could discover what worked best for both of us.

This is what the Master is seeking: common ground. Some women may have emotional, sexual, physical, or spiritual issues that may not surface until marriage, so it's important for men not to allow the frustration that can come with the infrequency of sex to creep into the conversation. A healthy environment must be created where a wife feels comfortable being honest with her husband about this issue. I guarantee having an environment like this will be a positive step to resolving whatever underlying issues there may be. A sex therapist or counselor may also need to be consulted. Don't be afraid to bring someone into your marriage who can help in this critical area. There are so many reasons why sex in marriage can become sporadic so don't be alarmed; stay committed to finding a healthy solution no matter how long it takes.

Create an Environment for Healing

By the time most women get to marriage, they've had to endure countless amounts of sexual, physical, emotional, and spiritual abuse at the hands of men. So marriage might be the first time in their life where they have the opportunity to heal from this abuse. It's important for husbands to be understanding and help create an environment in the marriage that can contribute to their wife's healing. One of the most effective ways to do this is through the power of service.

So much of what we are taught about marriage is how the woman should serve the man, but a man's marriage will go to the next level and healing can be fostered when men learn to serve their wives. Get to know her wants and needs, her likes and dislikes, her passions and pleasures. Then do everything in your power to serve those. The more a husband serves his wife, the more healing will take place. Why? Because many women have been taught love on a conditional basis. How many times have you heard the saying "the way to a man's heart is through his stomach"? Now, we all laugh when we hear that, but what gets ingrained in a woman's psyche is "in order for me to have love, I must do." The "doing" is then perceived as a condition to the receiving of love. So when a wife is served and it's not conditional, it's a powerful way for a husband to set the tone and make the healing of his wife a priority. The Master leads by love and service.

MASTERY IN CAREER

Mastery is a vital part of a successful career. One of the hottest debates any sports fan can engage in is who's the greatest basketball player of all time: LeBron James or Michael Jordan? It's very hard to get consensus on this question because there are so many differing opinions. However, most would agree that both men became masters at the game of basketball. They committed their professional lives to one pursuit and worked at it consistently.

Making a professional commitment to excellence and backing that up with integrity, hard work, and sacrifice is essential. Sometimes our lust for more—more money, more power, more responsibility—can blind us to how we go about achieving career advancement, and this type of lust can lead us to believe that the ends justify the means (which they don't).

For example, when I was an executive for Sony Pictures Entertainment, there was a time when my lust for more threatened to disrupt the Mastery I was trying to practice in my career. I talked a little about this in my book *The Hollywood Commandments*. I was developing the script for the remake of *The Karate Kid* and the producers had given me an early look at the first draft. I gave the script right to my boss; instead of giving it to my colleague, who was working on the project with me, I cut him out. And of course, my colleague found out. This moment functioned as an ethical mirror, and it made me look at myself and ask: *Is this who you really want to be? Backstabbing to get ahead? What kind of Master are you?*

I felt immediately remorseful and expressed my deep regret. I jeopardized my integrity for a moment of potential advancement and it didn't feel good at all. I let my lustful ambition get the best of me. My colleague was so angry that he went to our boss. I was contrite, owned up to my mistake, and told my boss it would never happen again. My saving grace was that I had built up a reputation of integrity on the job up to this point, so my boss gave me understanding and thankfully didn't hold this moment against me.

Practicing Mastery in our career means we must value integrity even more than advancement, because how we do what we do is more important than just doing it. Integrity absolutely matters.

History is filled with stories that illustrate how what we do in private matters—who we are when no one is watching—is who we really are, and real professional Mastery begins in the depths of our souls, not in a chair at the head of a boardroom table. To master any career, commit to knowing it fully. Commit to the process required to be successful, and resist the temptation to look for shortcuts. Masters don't play for speed; they play for true success, no matter how long it takes.

TO BE A MASTER, LOOK TO THE MASTER

Dear God, my Master, you created earth and sky by your great
power—by merely stretching out your arm! There is nothing
you can't do.

—JEREMIAH 32:17 (THE MESSAGE)

Obi-Wan Kenobi had Yoda. Rocky had Mickey Goldmill.
Daniel had Mr. Miyagi. Muhammad Ali had Angelo Dundee.
Michael Jordan had Phil Jackson. Steph Curry has Steve Kerr.
We have God. Every aspiring Master must submit to a greater
Master who can help teach him how to maximize his potential
and help him harness the power within.

Any power the Master in me has exists because I work
every day to submit myself to the true Master. Without submitting myself to God and His plan for my life, I'd be helpless
against the power of sin and the Dog. I can't tell you how many
times I've cried out to God to take this lust away, to take this
Dog out of me. Each time, I feel like His reply is similar to the
one Paul received: "My grace is sufficient for you." I relate one
thousand percent to how Paul detailed his battle with the Dog:

*If I had a mind to brag a little, I could probably do it without
looking ridiculous, and I'd still be speaking plain truth all the
way. But I'll spare you. I don't want anyone imagining me as
anything other than the fool you'd encounter if you saw me on
the street or heard me talk.*

*Because of the extravagance of those revelations, and so I
wouldn't get a big head, I was given the gift of a handicap to
keep me in constant touch with my limitations. Satan's angel
did his best to get me down; what he in fact did was push me
to my knees. No danger then of walking around high and
mighty! At first I didn't think of it as a gift, and begged God
to remove it. Three times I did that, and then he told me, "My
grace is enough; it's all you need. My strength comes into its
own in your weakness."*

*Once I heard that, I was glad to let it happen. I quit focus-
ing on the handicap and began appreciating the gift. It was
a case of Christ's strength moving in on my weakness. Now I
take limitations in stride, and with good cheer, these limitations that cut me down to size—abuse, accidents, opposition,
bad breaks. I just let Christ take over! And so the weaker I get,
the stronger I become.*

—2 Corinthians 12:6–10 (The Message)

Something powerful happens when we submit and accept
that we need God's help to sort through our feelings, short-
comings, and disappointments as men. Submission helps us get
back to God's original purpose: serving someone greater than
ourselves. The power of a Master is in selflessness, sacrifice, and
communicating with the true Master every day.

The 12-step program is used all over the world to help millions of people overcome their addictions to alcohol, sex, drugs,
gambling, and more. The program was introduced in 1939 in
the book *Alcoholics Anonymous: The Story of How Many Thou-*

sands of Men and Women Have Recovered from Alcoholism. It was primarily written by William G. Wilson—aka Bill W. He was a successful businessman but his life was in turmoil due to his alcoholism. He met a man named Dr. Bob through a support group and together they wrote the 12 steps that would become the essential core of the book, which, to date, has sold more than thirty million copies. The 12 steps start with: "We admitted we were powerless over alcohol [our addiction]—that our lives had become unmanageable."

Mastery is like the 12-step program: submitting to God is essential to succeed. When we bow our head and say, "Lord, who do you want me to be? Show me the way and help me not to fall prey to lust," that's not a sign of weakness but rather a sign of strength. Find the purpose of that service and Mastery will manifest. Remember, the Master can tap into his higher purpose: to fulfill his God-ordained purpose. While the Dog only serves his own pleasure, the Master can draw strength from someone and something much bigger than himself: God. Men, repeating the Master Affirmation daily will help you stay focused.

The Master Affirmation

I am fearfully and wonderfully made

I am powerful beyond belief

I have greatness within me

I have destiny ahead of me

I have creativity in my fingertips

I am honorable in a world of dishonor

I have integrity in each word I speak

I create value wherever I go

My purpose is bigger than my pain

I am committed in the face of chaos

I am courageous in the midst of battle

I am victorious over the war within

I am loved and I give love

I am . . . a Master

THE MASTER'S CREED

Ready are you? What know you of ready? . . . A Jedi must
have the deepest commitment, the most serious mind. This one
a long time have I watched. All his life has he looked away . . .
Adventure. Heh! Excitement. Heh! A Jedi craves not these
things. You are reckless!

—YODA, *THE EMPIRE STRIKES BACK*

Growing up, I remember being captivated by *Star Wars*, like so
many other people. Two of the aspects that fascinated me most
were the Force and the Jedi Master. That scene in *The Empire
Strikes Back* where Luke is on Dagobah with Yoda, trying to
learn how to master the Force, captivated my imagination. I
wanted to learn Jedi mind tricks that would give me the power
to lift objects with my thoughts! In short, I wanted to be a Jedi
Master. In my mind, there was no cooler aspiration. At the time
I had no idea I could become a Master in real life.

Outside the dog world, the term *master* is widely associated
with martial arts, and one of my favorite examples of a master
is the late Bruce Lee. Lee is often referred to as the greatest
martial artist of all time. Not only did he star in some of the
best martial arts films you will ever see (*Enter the Dragon* is my
favorite) but he also had motivational philosophies about self-
mastery that elevated him beyond just being an action star.

One of my favorite quotes of his is the following:

To me, ultimately, martial arts means honestly expressing yourself. Now, it is very difficult to do. It has always been very easy for me to put on a show and be cocky, and be flooded with a cocky feeling and feel pretty cool and all that. I can make all kinds of phony things. Blinded by it. Or I can show some really fancy movement. But to experience oneself honestly, not lying to oneself, and to express myself honestly, now that is very hard to do.

The martial arts master is an enduring icon in our culture because the ideal of the black belt embodies everything the Master stands for. A black belt is an indication of attainment of a high rank of skill in martial arts. To become a black belt in any martial arts form, you have to undergo years of training, with a belt test at each new rank. Earning a black belt can take years and thousands of hours of training. In order to progress to the point where they have the technical mastery, fitness, and skill to qualify for the black belt, students must develop discipline, precision, respect, and focus. At the same time, they are also required to teach younger students, encouraging them to develop patience and a calm mind.

All this culminates in the awarding of the black belt. But the student who receives the black belt is not merely a white belt that has learned to punch and kick with skill and power. Being a black belt is not about doing. He or she has changed—become stronger of mind, wiser, and more restrained. Wearing a black belt is about *being*. The distinguishing quality of the black belt is not the ability to beat someone else up in a fight, but the self-control and calm to not need to fight—the presence of mind to avoid trouble in the first place. That's why elder black belts are called "Master."

It's an honor to achieve a black belt in martial arts, but I believe an even greater achievement is to obtain one in the art of life. The practice of Mastery leads men to a level of attainment in life where our desire management skills become so powerful that we can master our urges, control our behavior, love with integrity, and lead with transparency. Practicing Mastery leads to peace-filled living because we gain skill in overcoming the desires that can sabotage us if we drop our guard.

Here are seven beliefs every Master should adhere to:

1. **Integrity.** The Master is the same man in private as he is in public. The values he espouses are the same ones he follows behind closed doors. He is a man of his word. He does what he says he will do and when he says that he adheres to a set of values, his actions back up his words. He sees some truths as self-evident: be truthful, keep your promises, be accountable for your mistakes, and try to make them right.

2. **Self-control.** The Master has his Dog on a tight leash at all times. His emotions are measured. He doesn't overreact or let passion overrule reason. On those rare occasions when his control of the Dog slips, he has safeties in place to get him back under control.

3. **Self-awareness.** The Master knows who he is, and he knows his strengths and weaknesses. He's fully aware of the triggers that make it difficult for him to be the man he wants to be.

He knows the type of people, environments, and situations that bring the worst out of him and he avoids them.

4. **Self-esteem.** The Master loves himself and is proud of who he is becoming. He deals with his brokenness honestly and doesn't need to chase after empty pleasure in order to feel good about himself. He's confident without being cocky.

5. **Humility.** The Master doesn't need to boast or show off in front of other men or women. In fact, he dislikes it. He's profoundly grateful for everyone and everything in his life and knows that not everyone is as blessed as he is, so he keeps everything in perspective. He doesn't have to make it all about him to be the Man.

6. **Leadership.** The Master sets an example for other men, not by his words but his actions. He doesn't need to lecture, because the peace and success of his life and relationships speak for themselves. But when other men come to him asking how he does it, he's more than willing to teach them.

7. **Faith.** The Master believes in the power of the unseen. Faith is substance of things hoped for, the evidence of things not seen. He has a vision for his life and the life of his family and he pursues it consistently.

BUILD A LEGACY

There is a call in the life of every man and woman. There is a destiny we are all designed to achieve.

Men, you have been made for greatness. The very essence of your being was created for success. But do you want your success to be disrupted because you could not get control of the Dog? Masters play for their legacy. It's not just about their life; it's about the life they will leave for others when their time on this earth is over.

Every man should ask himself "What type of legacy do I want to leave behind?" Will the legacy be the number of women he slept with? The number of cars or homes he bought? Mastery is about building a legacy that can be regarded with pride, one that inspires other men. What do you want to leave behind?

Think for a moment about hip-hop mogul Jay-Z. He was honest enough about the issues that he was facing as a man to address them. He decided he was going to do his work so that he could leave a legacy of commitment, fidelity, and love for his children. In his song "4:44" he raps, "I apologize, often womanize. Took for my child to be born, see through a woman's eyes." Our focus should not be just on what we do in this life for ourselves. It needs to be about the life we leave as an example for those who look to us to lead.

I wanted to create a pledge that basically functions as a mantra. The Master has a code, one that is designed to bring honor. If you are a man seeking to become better, I challenge you to take the Master's Pledge. If you are a woman reading this, challenge the men in your life (boyfriend, husband, brother, dad, son, friend) to take the Master's Pledge.

The Master's Pledge

- I pledge not to blame women for my actions. Women are never at fault when I lose control of the Dog. Nothing a woman wears, says, drinks, or does is an excuse for improper touching, remarks, or sexual behavior. *Ever.*

- I pledge to never harass a woman. Period.

- I pledge to stop looking the other way. If I witness a friend or colleague harassing a woman, I will say something.

- I pledge to stop making excuses for times when I behave badly. It's not the culture, peer pressure, porn, alcohol, or anything else. It's me.

- I pledge to confess my sins, apologize to whom I have offended, and live every day to make it right.

- I pledge to take a woman's "No" for an answer. No means no, period. It doesn't mean "Maybe." It doesn't mean "Try harder."

- I pledge to quit acting like my manhood is an entitlement for sex. It's not.

- I pledge to get the help I need if I struggle with anger or violence. I have to break the cycle of physical, psychological, and emotional abuse among men.

- I pledge to change my routine. If there's any part of my routine that makes me vulnerable to being less than I know I can be, I must change it.

- I pledge to take accountability for who I am and what I do. What I will be I am now becoming.

CHAPTER 4

DON'T FEED THE DOG

A grandfather is talking with his grandson and he says there
are two wolves inside of us that are always at war with each
other. One of them is a good wolf that represents things like
kindness, bravery, and love. The other is a bad wolf, which
represents things like greed, hatred, and fear. The grandson
stops and thinks about it for a second, then he looks up at his
grandfather and says, "Grandfather, which one wins?" The
grandfather quietly replies, "The one you feed."

—"THE TALE OF TWO WOLVES"

Elisabeth Geier, a dog enthusiast and blogger for *The Dog
People*, wrote a post called "The Truth About Dog Food—
An Exposé Every Dog Lover Needs to Read." In the post
she talked about going into her local pet supply store to buy the
brand of dog food she often bought for her two pit bulls. She
couldn't find it, and asked the owner where she could find it.
To her surprise, the store owner said they didn't recommend
the brand any longer. A large corporation had bought the company and changed its food safety standards, and as a result the

store decided to stop carrying the brand. "I was shocked," Elisabeth wrote. "I had been feeding my dogs this brand for several years, assuming it was fine, but I hadn't known the full story."

This isn't so different from us, really. So many times we feed ourselves things that are detrimental to our overall health because we don't always know the full story behind what we're eating and how what we eat can negatively impact our mental, spiritual, and physical well-being.

"The Tale of Two Wolves" has been repeated for generations, yet no one knows the exact origin. Some attribute it to Native American lore, others to the playwright George Bernard Shaw, and some even believe it originated with the Reverend Billy Graham (who wrote a variation of this story in his 1978 book *The Holy Spirit*). But even with its origins unknown, the truth of the story is the reason it has endured.

In the context of our conversation about the Dog and the Master, the answer to the question "Which one wins?" is the same. The one we feed. It's simple cause and effect. If we feed the Dog, the Master will starve. If we feed the Master, the Dog will starve.

The battle over feeding the Dog versus feeding the Master is waged every day. It's easy to feed the Dog, and often we do it without thinking. At times I've struggled to feed the Master in me more than I feed the Dog. Most men face this struggle. What I've come to learn is whichever one I feed is the one that will win the battle to control my behavior. When the Master is malnourished, he doesn't have the strength to rein in the Dog, because the Dog is overfed and has grown stronger.

Famed dog whisperer César Millán talks about what we should do when our dogs overeat in his post "Why dogs eat . . . and eat . . . and eat . . .": "As a Pack Leader, your job is to provide protection and direction. If your dog suddenly starts overeating, then you need to determine the cause, then take the behavioral or medical steps necessary to solve the problem." The same goes for men. When the Dog is getting fed more than the Master, we have to take the necessary steps to correct this diet and put the Master back in control.

Even though I'll often be referencing men as I lay out the difference between virtue and vice in this section, please understand that much of this knowledge is relevant for women too. Men aren't the only ones who struggle with vice. Women, as you read this, don't be afraid to wear the shoe as it fits.

SOUL FOOD VERSUS DOG FOOD

> You proceeded to eat it 'cause you was in the mood
> But Holmes you did not read it was a can of dog food!
> —RUN-DMC

You've heard the saying "You are what you eat." What we put into our bodies is what our bodies become. If we eat healthy, chances are we will enjoy high energy and good health for years to come. If we fill our body with junk food, processed foods, and excess sugar, then chances are we will have poorer health as we get older.

There are two types of food that feed our spirit. I call them *Soul food* and *Dog food*. The Master is fueled by Soul food; Dog food fuels the Dog.

The main ingredient in Soul food is *virtue*.
The main ingredient in Dog food is *vice*.

Virtue is behavior that reflects high moral standards such as righteousness, integrity, dignity, honor, decency, respectability, and faith. A virtue draws on and reinforces the highest moral qualities: authenticity, honesty, integrity, courage, self-control, wisdom, compassion, and mindfulness. Simply put, if it makes you better in body, mind, and spirit, it's a virtue.

Vice is anything that contributes to behavior that makes our will submissive to the appetites of lust. Vice is any habit that is physically, mentally, emotionally, or spiritually harmful. Frequent indulgence in harmful, immoral, sinful, or degrading practices is vice in action. A vice draws on and reinforces the lowest moral qualities: vanity, vulgarity, impulsiveness, arrogance, perversion, and selfishness. Vices can deaden us to normal emotional exchanges and the pleasures of love and romance: the gentle touch, the slow dance, the loving kiss. After a while, only pleasure in its crudest forms matters. Vice is like junk food for the soul, making the recipient potentially ethically, emotionally, mentally, and sometimes biologically unhealthy.

The choice between virtue and vice is an ongoing struggle. Why? Because consuming vice feels *good*. Indulging in vices brings immediate gratification, momentary stress relief, a feeling of careless fun, and an experience of losing our inhibitions. Remember, the Dog only cares about the pursuit of pleasure. Like a pet dog, which will keep gulping down food as long as you put it in the bowl until it makes itself sick, lust will keep devouring pleasure after pleasure until it sickens the spirit. Vices are addictive pleasures.

Vices have an impact on our behavior similar to how junk food works on our brain. Our brains can come to crave salt, sugar, and fat in the same way the brain can crave drugs. *Healthline* says, "Processed junk foods have a powerful effect on the 'reward' centers in the brain, involving brain neurotransmitters like dopamine. The foods that seem to be the most problematic include typical 'junk foods,' as well as foods that contain either sugar or wheat, or both." Once we develop a taste for bad food and regularly consume it, our dependency can become so strong that it's hard to quit eating it. That's why so many of us have such a difficult time giving up things that are terrible for us.

Overeating, drinking too much, smoking, doing drugs, promiscuous sex—these are just a few specific examples of vices that are destructive and highly addictive. Sometimes the hunger for these vices and many others becomes stronger than the hunger for virtue; that's one of the reasons why anyone can find him- or herself giving in to vices and going back to bad behaviors (and people) time after time even though we know they aren't good for us. Give in to vices enough and they become a prison that is hard to escape.

Vice is food for the Dog because every exposure to vice encourages our worst instincts. Vices appeal to our primitive, animal nature, especially to men's animal nature. Any time men act in a way that mindlessly services lust, that's a sign of engaging in vice and feeding the Dog. Engaging in vice feeds the Dog and makes it stronger until the Dog feels entitled to a feast whenever it wants.

The secret to overcoming our vices is to understand the power of temptation. We can only be tempted by what we want. Temptation is powerful. It's hard to turn away from it. But we have to talk about it. That's what enables us to take away its power.

For example, let's look at an extreme version of this: the world of strip clubs. This culture dominates hip-hop music, so much so that many top artists pay strip clubs to play their music. Songs glorifying strip club culture have been regular fixtures atop the Billboard charts, from "I'm in Love with a Stripper" to "Bandz a Make Her Dance" to "Rake It Up." How much money a man can afford to blow at a strip club has become a vice-driven status symbol. The Internet is littered with videos and social media posts of men "making it rain," with one man trying to outdo the last. It's been reported that the boxer Floyd Mayweather once spent $100,000 at a strip club in one night!

The influence of strip clubs is more pervasive than you may think. I've been to a strip club twice in my life. Once was for a friend's bachelor party when I was in my early twenties; the other was around the same time during a trip to Hawaii.

I personally don't understand the allure. What's the point of being aroused by a woman just for the purpose of that arousal? What's the point of throwing hard-earned money up in the air on a woman dancing? Be that as it may, strip club culture has become a normalized part of male behavior that most men just accept. But that's an environment where vices thrive and the Dogs in men are given more food than they know what to do with. And it's this vice—aka the Dog food diet—that is doing more harm to men than most even realize.

Jan Rockwell, a licensed mental health professional, says that many men who attend "strip clubs struggle with communication and intimacy with their wives or partners, which can promote a secret life." She goes on to say that "a secret life also changes the neurochemistry in the brain." Did you catch that? Going to strip clubs as part of a secret life and keeping it from the women in your life can actually change your brain! Believe me—the harm and danger are very real.

Let's look at a lighter example of prevalent vice: reality TV. From VH1's *Love & Hip Hop* to *The Real Housewives* franchise to even *The Bachelor*, vice is on full display on these shows. From fights to cheating, to drinking too much, to fantasy romance and sex, vice powers most of television's successful reality TV programs. To underscore the addictive nature of vice, consider that these shows are some of the highest-rated and longest-running shows on TV. Dr. Bryan Gibson of Central Michigan University conducted a study and found that watching reality shows can make people more aggressive. He recently told Tess Vigeland, guest host of NPR's *All Things Considered*,

"We knew from past research that people who see relational aggression in media tend to become more aggressive." Vice pulls our focus away from *being* and puts it on *doing*. It can turn a man into someone who pursues quick pleasure at any cost. It can kill foresight and long-term thinking.

The only way to loosen vice's grip on our lives is to stop feeding it. Whatever you want more of in life, feed it—it will grow. Whatever you want to have less of, starve. It will become weaker. If you want love, respect, peace, and happiness, then you must try to devour virtue consistently. Virtue is the true Soul food.

Virtue fills us up. It makes us *more*: more compassionate, more courageous, more loving, more self-aware. The more men consume virtue, the more it helps them maintain consistency in public and in private. What you feed your spirit in private will nourish the persona that shows up in public. Virtue helps take behavior out of the shadows and into the light.

One of the reasons I'm so passionate about this is because I've seen the destructive power of vice in my life. My father was an alcoholic. He regularly smoked weed and cigarettes, and ate food high in salt, dying at thirty-six from a massive heart attack. He spent the majority of his time on this earth letting his vices get the best of him, and as a result, my brothers and I have had to navigate life without a father. I recently found out that his parents were both alcoholics, which explains why most of my uncles have struggled with alcoholism and drug abuse. The Dog's hunger for vice is so strong that it will not stop until it destroys everything in its wake. I live every day with the remnants of the destruction that vice can inflict on a family. That's what makes me so committed to helping as many people as I can, especially men, overcome its power.

I believe most men want to live on a diet of virtue. I told some of the men in my life that I was writing this book and they got very excited. Guys who were as young as their twenties told me, "Yes! This is what we need! Someone needs to talk about what men go through so it's out in the open!"

Women reading this, believe me when I say that many men do want to be honorable and faithful. It may not always seem like it, but they do. Sometimes they just need your help to get there. Many men are terrified of talking to others about their greatest struggle because they don't want to be judged or seen as weak, so it never gets discussed openly. There are millions of men right now who want to turn away from a diet of vice to one of virtue, yet it's a struggle, and they don't know how to make the change.

VICE IS CELEBRATED

In "Your Kids Are Surrounded by Junk Food. So What's a Parent to Do?," a blog post on *Today's Parent*, Sarah Elton talks about how hard it is for parents to feed their kids healthy food when there is so much food that is bad for them everywhere our kids look—school lunches, birthday parties, etc. Parents trying to feed their children healthy food face a similar problem to men trying to live a healthy life: junk food—like vice—is everywhere.

One of the main reasons it's such a struggle to live virtuously is because vice is all around us. Our culture not only tolerates vice, but celebrates it. As noted above, just look at the success of reality TV, which is primarily a vice-driven category of television. How many of these shows right now are based on fighting, excess, and straight-up lust? There have been many times when I have pitched unscripted programming based around virtuous themes and watched the executives *literally* roll their eyes. No one wants to watch people behaving well, they seem to be saying. There's no money in that. And let's be honest: promoting vice *can* make you rich; just look at the world of hip-hop.

Once upon a time, hip-hop truly was an art form focused on empowerment, yet it has been taken over by vice-driven music. However, even if the music does make some people rich, it does not justify the personal and cultural damage it causes. For example, here's a line from G-Eazy, A$AP Rocky, and Cardi B's hit song, "No Limit": "F**k him then I get some money." Also, in Future's hit song "Mask Off" there is a repeated chant about the dangerous drugs "Molly" and Percocet. Hip-hop culture is so vice addicted and ready to promote vice that even talking about this will get me criticized. I'm all about artistic freedom, and whoever has the microphone is free to talk about whatever they please, whether we agree with it or not. I'm not anti-hip-hop; I love the music.

However, I see so many young people killing their potential because vice-filled music has a hold on their minds, telling them how they're supposed to live. The culture doesn't seem to care what the message is, as long as the beat is hot or as long as people stream it. Why? Money. Hip-hop and popular culture are dependent on feeding the Dog to make a profit. This is why the music is so prevalent. But the collateral damage is that it's harming the potential of young women and destroying the Master in men, black and white, young and old.

Men and women, please, don't just follow any culture (hip-hop or otherwise) mindlessly and become what it wants you to be. As the Message translation of Romans 12:2 says, "Don't become so well-adjusted to your culture that you fit into it without even thinking." We do have the capability of putting songs, TV shows, and movies filled with vice in the proper perspective so they don't entice our lust. But that can only happen when we acknowledge the culture for what it really is and make the choice to rise above it. Don't let the content control you or distort what we know to be true: virtue is the path to life, and vice can be the road to death.

VIRTUE IS RESISTED

People often mistake virtue for being boring. Men, making Soul food your diet doesn't mean sitting at home every night or spending your vacations in a museum or your spare time in a library. There's nothing about being the Master or pursuing a life of virtue that says you can't enjoy everything from sports to great music, to great food and great experiences. Being the Master and feeding on virtue simply means you enjoy those things in the context of your higher self, with discipline, self-awareness, respect, and honor. You're still you, just with the best parts dialed up. Believe me, the woman in your life will appreciate the difference (and if you don't have a woman in your life, this difference will help attract her).

However, when a man talks about wanting to live a virtuous life, he must be prepared for people to look at him like he's crazy. Misery loves company, so if a man sees another man wanting to better himself, he may try to sabotage him. Some men can mock other men who take the path of virtue, calling them boring, weak, a wimp, a killjoy, a wuss, a goody two-shoes, a square, or "holier than thou." They may ask, "Do you think you're better than me?" I wish I could tell you how many times other men have called me names for wanting to live with virtue. It's too many to count.

Men, you know this if you've ever been with a group of guys that couldn't wait to hit the town and go drinking, partying, and chasing after women, but said you weren't into it. Maybe you decided the whole scene was immature or you were just tired from a long workweek. You probably experienced what usually happens when someone tries to steer the night away from vice toward virtue. There's peer pressure to "man up." They try to get you to stop being a coward and to be game for anything. If you still refuse, the Dog in them can even get angry, as though your refusal to go along with the pack means you're judging them. Dogs are pack animals, and pack animals hunt and feed in groups. The Dogs in men can act the same way. Vice draws strength from numbers, which is why you can see guys chasing vice while roaming around in groups. Somehow, if other men around them are doing it, it doesn't feel as bad to let the Dog out.

If a man suddenly decides to stop clubbing and sleeping around, or refuses an invitation to go to Vegas with the fellas, there will probably be some pushback. It could get ugly. One of the realities of allowing the Master to take control of a man is that a man can become a mirror to other men who are still letting the Dog run free. So if they look at that man and don't like what they see in themselves, they might snarl. It's a false self-defense mechanism.

That is part of the price of Mastery. It's also a great way to screen friends and figure out who is really meant to be one. If a man wants to be a Master, that man should hang with other men who want him to be happy and who aspire to Mastery themselves. The men who want to keep feeding on Dog food so they can feel less guilty are not worth the time of the man who wants to live differently.

Men, you have to make the decision about the type of man, husband, boyfriend, father, and friend you want to be. Virtue is the path that can take you to a place where you can successfully sustain the person you want to be, but you have to be purposeful about it.

At first I was offended when I was ridiculed by other men, and I was tempted to act in a way that would show those guys I was anything but a square or a goody-goody. But then I thought, *What good would that do me?* Only I would suffer for living the way they wanted me to live.

I also came to see that ridicule was just praise in disguise. I would ask myself, "What's goody-two-shoes about wanting the best for your life without compromising your peace or damaging your soul?" If that's the definition of being a "goody," then so be it. I'm grateful for the haters, then and now; they only make me stronger and they will only make you stronger as well.

Resist the temptation to live down to other people's expectations. Let them call you what they want, but don't let it deter you from becoming who you know you were created to be. Set the bar high and push yourself to get the most out of life. Embrace the ridicule you might face, because the end result is worth it.

THE VICE VERSUS VIRTUE DIET

The more we engage in virtuous behaviors, the faster we develop our best qualities. It isn't just that vice can get us in trouble while virtue keeps us out of it. That's just the tip of the iceberg. The real issue here is that as with anything, what we consume or practice contributes to who we are becoming. A diet of vice, a diet of virtue—both change us. It's just a question of whether we're changing into the person we want to be or the person we don't want to become.

A Vice diet is enticing because it's easy. It's easy for someone to give themselves over to a sexual frenzy or drown their fears in alcohol. Vice can provide instant gratification.

Vice is like a binge. Virtue is a practice.

Virtue is harder because it takes work. Yet virtue is like a muscle: the more it's used, the stronger it becomes. A Soul food diet can produce incredible, positive change in a man. I have been deliberately feeding myself Soul food and working to eliminate Dog food for a long time, and while I'm not perfect, I've seen the improvements a diet like this can produce in my life.

A Virtue diet feeds the Master; a Vice diet feeds the Dog. Virtue provides energy and vitality and builds discipline, integrity, fidelity, strength, and compassion. Vice creates recklessness, negativity, and weakness and tears down your self-control, peace, and purpose.

So what does feeding the Master look like? What does feeding the Dog look like?

A Soul food diet is any consistent consumption of virtue that includes but is not limited to the following:

- **Health and Fitness.** Get regular exercise, eat a healthy diet, and get enough sleep.
- **Prayer.** Speaking to God every day is a powerful way to stay focused and aligned. Prayer changes things.
- **Meditation.** Find time each day to calm your mind; focus on breathing, relax, and stop reliving the past or worrying about the future. Meditation has proven positive benefits for the brain and the mind.
- **Consuming high-quality entertainment.** Watch or listen to content that helps strengthen and edify the mind. This type of content can still give us an escape, but doesn't trigger negative vices.

- **Reading great books.** Spend time reading material that elevates the mind. It doesn't matter if it's self-help, a great thriller, a classic, or a piece of nonfiction. Great books feed the soul.

- **Practicing empathy.** Practice regarding others not with scorn and judgment but with compassion and understanding.

- **Spending time with family and friends.** Invest time in quality relationships (e.g., spouse, girlfriend, children, friends who bring out the best in you).

- **Service.** Help others, whether that means mentoring or serving at church or a community organization. Being of service to others is gratifying.

- **Generosity.** Be quicker to give than to ask for something. Do things for people without asking for anything in return.

- **Church.** Guidance, leadership, and fellowship among the right group of people can be transformative.

- **Reading Scripture.** Make time every week to study. You will find new insights, even in passages you thought you knew well.

The Dog food diet is any consistent consumption of vice. It includes but is not limited to the following:

- **Promiscuous sex.** Sleeping with an endless string of women.

- **Deceptiveness.** Cheating on your wife or girlfriend.

- **Power.** Pursuing power only to satisfy the ego, especially if it means betraying values, family, or even doing something illegal.
- **Greed.** When getting more for its own sake becomes an obsession.
- **Drinking too much.** Excessive drinking and losing control is dangerous. Anything that blunts our ability to have self-control is a license for lust to take over.
- **Drug use.** Any kind of substance that changes how someone feels, impairs their judgment, and alters their perception of reality.
- **Overeating or eating food that is bad for you.** We all struggle with eating things that might taste good but aren't good for our system. A healthy diet is key to a healthy life.
- **Constant use of social media.** Spending countless hours on social media can be unhealthy emotionally, spiritually, and physically. It can also become a distraction from the things you want to focus your mind on.
- **Pornography.** As I've noted, pornography is a huge problem and an addiction for many men. This is one of the most secret yet most common vices.
- **Some forms of entertainment.** As discussed, certain types of music, movies, and TV shows can promote vice.
- **Prostitution.** Prostitution turns sex into nothing more than a transaction empty of emotion or commitment.

Men, the same way it takes time, practice, and commitment to learn how to master the Dog, it takes time to learn how to get vice out of our system. Put yourself on a low vice diet! You might not be able to go cold turkey, but you can begin to reduce your dependence on your vices right now by limiting their consumption gradually until you get to the point where you no longer are dependent on them.

Don't half step. We can't dine on virtue but eat vice for a midnight snack. Consistency is king. When we go out into the world and behave in a way that displays courage, honor, compassion, restraint, discipline, steadfastness, and integrity, it gets easier to do so again the next day. Every day it gets a little easier. Every day you make progress you become more reluctant to give back. This is a process; so don't beat yourself up if you find yourself falling back into certain vices that you have committed to overcoming. Get back up, ask for forgiveness, and keep going. It takes a lifetime to master the Dog, so just because you want to live virtuously doesn't mean the desire for vice goes away. However, over time you'll see that you have more strength and a better game plan to manage those desires.

After a while, you will start to feel proud about the man you are becoming. Your relationships with women will become more open, honest, and respectful. Your relationships with men will become more mature and caring. Opportunities will open to you, and you won't miss the toxic people and behaviors you've cut out of your life. You'll love who you're becoming. And that's what it's all about.

So stop. Today. *Now*. Stop feeding the Dog. Change your plans, delete those apps, block those numbers. Go out into the world and start behaving in a way that reflects the qualities of

Mastery that you want to bring into your life, and you will become those qualities.

Women, I want to avoid laying any responsibility for changing men at your feet. However, when it comes to the question of Soul food versus Dog food, men need your help creating a vice-free environment. If you're in a situation with a man who's sincerely trying to become his best self, help him out by putting Dog food out of reach. If you're the mother of a son, please make sure you feed him the Virtue diet; it truly will feed his soul.

WHAT ARE YOU EATING?

Take a look at what's on your plate right now. Check the ones that apply to you.

Vice

☐ 1. I drink to excess or use drugs regularly.

☐ 2. I party constantly.

☐ 3. I regularly have more than one sex partner.

☐ 4. I regularly lie to get ahead professionally.

☐ 5. I buy things I can't afford to compete with other people.

☐ 6. I compete with other people as a way to achieve personal validation.

☐ 7. I continuously flirt even though I'm married or in a relationship.

☐ 8. I'm addicted to social media.

Virtue

☐ 1. I regularly make myself of service to others.

☐ 2. I say no when my friends propose activities that don't align with my spirit.

☐ 3. I don't drink to excess (or at all) and I don't use drugs.

☐ 4. I'm currently in a monogamous, committed relationship.

☐ 5. I meditate and pray regularly.

☐ 6. I live a healthy lifestyle and eat a healthy diet.

☐ 7. I read consistently to educate and improve myself.

☐ 8. I help build community with other people in my life.

How many did you check? If your Vice checks outnumbered your Virtue checks by three or more, you're eating too much vice. If your Virtue checks beat your Vice checks by three or more, you're eating virtue. If you're about even, then you're finding your way but can make changes today that will get you on the right path.

CHAPTER 5

CLAIM YOUR TERRITORY

When you love someone you protect them from the pain, you
don't become the cause of it.

—UNKNOWN

If you don't want temptation to follow you, don't act as if
you're interested.

—RICHARD L. EVANS

Dogs love to push boundaries because they're always trying to discover how much they can get away with. One of the areas in which dogs often exhibit bad behavior is encroaching on their owner's personal space—jumping up, pawing at them, sitting at their feet, leaning against their leg, nipping at them, or following them around.

Dog trainer Cheri Lucas teaches about the need for strong body language, eye contact, and commanding energy to get dogs to respect their owner and their owner's personal space. The door, couch, food, toys, and key areas of the house are all considered extensions of personal space. In other words, per-

sonal space is basically territory. Dog owners must claim their
territory or their dogs will claim it themselves.

As we've discussed, the lust in men is strong, and when
its territory is challenged, it can act like an aggressive dog. An
aggressive dog wants what it wants and wants to go where it
wants to go. It will act out if challenged. In order to reclaim
territory, many dog trainers recommend using a calm, assertive
energy to communicate control and let the dog know you have
no fear. They also recommend adjusting body language to communicate to a dog "I am going to own the space I'm in." When
a dog senses this shift in authority, many times the dog calms
down and begins the process of learning to respect the owner's
territory.

The most effective way to gain respect, which is key to
claiming an owner's territory, is to set boundaries.

Where there are no boundaries there can be no respect.

This is not only true for dogs and their owners, but also in
life! Boundaries help us maintain a level of respect in any
relationship or friendship we're in. Respect is critical to ensure
the health of any relationship. Boundaries help keep threats
to the relationship at bay and provide protection to those
within the relationship or friendship. In my experience advis-
ing people over the years, I've noticed that boundary setting is
an area where most people struggle. The tricky thing is that
you often don't notice that firm boundaries haven't been set
until it's too late. You've fallen into a pattern of behavior that

doesn't protect the things or people dear to you, and it's hard to speak up and set them after the fact.

Healthy relationships (in dating and marriage) are the foundation of a healthy society. However, the Dog has caused tremendous damage in this area, and we can see this damage in the cheating, infidelity, and divorces that are so common in our society. In order to win the battle over the Dog, we have to create strong boundaries. When we don't create strong boundaries, we often suffer as a result. In this chapter, I will talk about how to protect and safeguard relationships from the ways of the Dog and reclaim territory that might have previously been lost as a result of weak boundaries.

DON'T LET ANYONE CAMP IN YOUR YARD

Men and women, think about your relationship with your significant other (whether in marriage or a committed relationship) as your yard. My yard is my life with Meagan—not just our home life, but also our emotional and spiritual life as husband and wife. Because of our demanding schedules we're apart a lot—she might be shooting a movie or TV show on location, or I might be producing a movie or traveling for a speaking engagement—so it's important we make sure that even when we are not together, we have safeguards in place to protect our yard. One of our most important safeguards is not allowing anyone else to fulfill our emotional needs.

Just as the allure of a real yard is found in the beauty of its landscaping, the beauty of a relationship is found in the depth of its emotional intimacy. In an article for *Psychology Today* Linda and Charlie Bloom define *emotional intimacy* as a closeness and connection that "requires a high level of transparency and openness" that "involves a degree of vulnerability," and they go on to say that "[c]ouples who engage in this level of connectivity enjoy a sense of being at peace within themselves and with each other. . . . All this adds up to a formula for enhanced emotional well-being, and physical health as well." In other words, you have to be vulnerable and connected to have a strong relationship.

But emotional intimacy is dangerous too because it's not like physical intimacy. It's pretty clear if you're sleeping with another woman or kissing someone behind your girlfriend's back. But emotional intimacy is trickier to recognize. It might start with sharing confidences over a work lunch. It could be telling your guy friend things you don't open up to your husband about. Maybe you start to feel connected to this other person in a way you used to feel connected to your spouse. It's easy to justify or rationalize the behavior away. It's just lunch; you're just talking to a friend. You're not cheating on anyone. It's easy to become emotionally intimate with someone before you realize how deep you're in it.

Emotional intimacy is a gateway to a better relationship, but it can also be a path toward infidelity. Emotional intimacy is a need, whether we know it or not. We will find ourselves attracted—emotionally, spiritually, and physically—to whomever meets our emotional needs. Letting another person who is not your monogamous partner get a foothold on emotional intimacy in your life is like letting someone camp out in your front yard.

Men, if a woman who is not your significant other is meeting any of your emotional needs, you are courting chaos and potential disaster. Letting another woman occupy a place of emotional intimacy in your life is a danger zone. It's an invitation to trouble, because it's a short mental leap from "Wow, I can really talk to her about my issues and she really seems to care" to "Wow, I feel so connected, maybe this is where I'm supposed to be." And we all know where that leads. If a man wants to put the Master in control, his yard must be protected at all times. An outsider shouldn't be allowed to come into our yard and set up house.

Men, if you are experiencing this problem, first things first. Stop lying to yourself: if you're finding yourself powerfully drawn to another woman because she seems to "get" you and care about your needs, that's a giant red flag that there's a potential deficit in your current relationship. Don't romanticize this other woman and pretend she's suddenly your soul mate.

Next, talk to your wife or girlfriend honestly about your emotional needs. If you're not getting everything you need from your relationship, chances are neither is she, so it's important to discuss how you can both do things differently and how you can both become better at meeting each other's needs. Whether that means changing your schedules so you have more intimate time together, getting counseling, or something else, do it. And keep your yard clear by making a clean break from the woman who's been complicit in what qualifies as emotional cheating.

Yes, *emotional* cheating. If you're sharing something deeply personal with someone who's not your significant other, it doesn't matter if you never touch each other. Emotional intimacy is still a violation. It's a test drive for the real thing. It's illicit, exciting, addictive, and a trap. It won't end well. If you keep getting closer and closer, and you tell yourself "you've got this," then sooner or later you will end up crossing the line and potentially having to invest a lifetime repairing the emotional damage you've inflicted on your significant other. So end it with the "friend" and start talking to your wife or girlfriend. Get your needs met at home and keep your yard clean.

Dr. Shauna Springer, a licensed psychologist and founder of Hidden Ivy Consulting, says: "What happens is in a solid healthy marital dynamic there's kind of like a wall around the couple and the relationship, and they have a window into each other's hearts and souls, and they know each other and have a deeper intimacy than they have with anybody outside the marriage. . . . What happens in the dynamics of an affair . . . is that one of the partners opens up a window in that wall to somebody outside the relationship. They start disclosing things outside of the relationship, and they start building this inappropriate bond. Whether it's sexual or emotional, it's a window into the marriage. They say things like, 'You make me feel ways that my partner doesn't.' Even in a healthy relationship, there's that kind of discourse with affair partners."

Women, be careful if a man who you know is married or in

a relationship is allowing you to fulfill his emotional needs. Just as he can become vulnerable to you, you can become vulnerable to him, because you can begin to feel a sense of deep connection when you share intimate details from your lives. Be on guard; this can happen much easier than you think. It can start off casually and innocently, yet snowball quickly into something significant. I'm not talking about casual conversation. I'm talking about when you find yourself discussing details of the man's relationship with him, hearing about his discontent with his wife or girlfriend, or hearing him talk about his loneliness. This is when you both are entering the danger zone. If you are reading this and you know you're in this situation with a man, you need to get yourself out. If you can, call him out and bring the situation to light, but don't allow him to use you like this any longer. The same way you wouldn't want someone messing in your yard, resist the temptation to do the same in someone else's. You'll be protecting him and yourself.

Ladies, it's also your right to call your man on any relation-ships he has with women that seem inappropriate. He might think you're being a nag or unnecessarily suspicious, but that's okay—you protect what you care about. Your yard must be se-cured. If he's spending a lot of time talking to another woman, even if he insists they're just friends, call him on it. Nothing good can come of a man going outside your relationship to get his emotional needs met. If you're worried because you fear this is happening to you, talk to him about his female friends. But keep in mind, tone is everything, as I've noted, so don't come at him as if he's already guilty. Try to maintain a tone of love and respect. If he becomes evasive or angry, don't allow this to upset you, stay calm and persist. Ask until you get clear answers, because it's possible the friendship has created a blind spot for him. He might need you to point out how and where the friendship is unhealthy. Protect your yard vigilantly.

Oh, and men, the same goes for you. You know how easy it is for men to allow the Dog to be in control, so be mindful of the men your wife or girlfriend spends time with. This isn't a call for controlling, jealous, or chauvinistic behavior—quite the opposite. It's just a call to be sensitive about your relationship and protective of it in a healthy way. The same way you could have a blind spot about a female friendship, she could have one about male friendships. If you feel uneasy about one of her male friendships, talk to her about it in a calm, nonjudgmental manner. What you bring up could be a false alarm, or it could be a legitimate issue; either way, communication is key to sorting through all these concerns in a positive and productive way.

Lastly, some advice for married couples. Meagan and I have a rule we live by: don't discuss your marriage problems with your single friends. Unfortunately, in our experience, single friends truly have no idea what it takes to make a marriage work. As a result, they can inadvertently become a source of really poor advice. Don't let single friends camp out in your yard by giving you advice that could be detrimental to your marriage. Find a good married couple, preferably one that's been married for longer than you have, that you can seek wisdom from.

BUILD A BETTER FENCE

Good fences make good neighbors.

—ROBERT FROST, "MENDING WALL"

There's a hilarious YouTube video of a guy who went out of his way to build a beautiful new fence to keep his dog, Stella, from getting into his neighbor's yard. In the eighteen-second video, he stands back, filming the moment he reveals the new fence. He says, "Yep, just completed fixing this fence. Pretty proud of it, I'd have to say. Try to keep Stella in the yard." Then a second later, here comes Stella, who jumps right over the fence! His response is a resigned "Dammit." He thought the fence would be high enough to contain her, but unfortunately he was wrong and had to go back to the drawing board.

Here's another funny but absolutely true story. It's from Annie Greer's hilarious book *The Chimp Who Loved Me*. Annie and her veterinarian husband, Kent, operate several animal clinics in central Florida, and years ago a man brought his sick Doberman pinscher to be looked at. After examining the dog, Kent said he thought the dog had swallowed a foreign object and would need surgery to remove it. The man agreed and left his dog at the clinic overnight.

Later that day, Kent operated on the dog and, as expected, found a foreign object twisted up in its digestive tract: a pair of red Victoria's Secret panties. Kent removed them, stitched the Doberman up, and called the man to tell him his dog was going to be fine and he could take him home the next day.

The next morning the man showed up at the clinic . . . with his wife. (Don't get ahead of me.) Kent brought them into the recovery room so they could see the dog, and then showed the couple the panties that had caused the blockage. Icily, the woman said, "I don't shop at Victoria's Secret." If the scene had been from a reality show that would have been the moment when the camera zoomed in on the husband's horrified face while his wife went crazy on him. What really happened was that the couple ended up getting a divorce—and the wife got the dog!

When a man is allowing the Master in him to be in control, he must always think ahead. He's got to be prepared, building the right type of fence so that fence thwarts the Dog, so to speak. So let's talk about how to build fences.

Fences are built for protection and privacy and to keep out anything or anybody who might pose a threat. It's important to build a better fence—or maybe to build a fence for the first time—for your relationship. It's surprising how few people sit down and talk about how to protect their relationship. We live in a world where there's insurance for everything from cell phones to cars to jewelry. Just in case something happens to our stuff, we have it covered. But if we have protection for material things that are replaceable, why wouldn't we put greater protections—aka fences—in place to safeguard our relationships, which are irreplaceable?

Let's be clear: Fences aren't designed to put restrictions on the relationship. They are made to do the opposite, to establish more safety within the relationship. When we feel safe inside a relationship, it actually creates more freedom for us to be who we really are, because we know we have the love, support, and acceptance of the one we're with.

Invisible electric fences are widely used to keep dogs from going out of or into yards where they do not belong. Many people are not fans because of the potential harm to a dog from the electric shock when they venture too far. Be that as it may, the fences that can help make your relationship flourish operate in a similar way. They are invisible, so others won't know they exist, but you know they are there. Every relationship is different, so you have to choose the fence that works best for your relationship. However, here are a few I recommend.

Phone Usage and Social Media Boundaries

Phones and social media are creating havoc in so many relationships because they are a major communication disruptor. Relationships (including marriages) are being broken down one scroll at a time. It's so easy to check out of a relationship and check into an alternate world of likes, swipes, posts, and memes. According to Deloitte, the average adult checks their phone forty-seven times a day, eighty-nine percent of cell phone users check their phone within an hour of waking up. Eighty-one percent check their phones in the hour before they go to sleep. These stats are just the tip of the iceberg. The danger this presents is multifaceted.

Constantly being on your phone while you're with your partner is an intimacy killer. As I've discussed, emotional intimacy is essential for a successful relationship. Using our phones can do untold damage because we can find ourselves so distracted that we aren't completely plugging into our significant other in a concentrated, distraction-free way. I admit there have been times Meagan has had to get on me about being on my phone when we're at home trying to spend quality time together. Somehow I find myself turning to it for no real reason. When I've been at work all day and then come home and pay attention to my phone instead of my wife, it sends a message: the world inside my phone is more important than you right now. It's important to not let anything disturb the connection and communication in your relationship, including—and especially—your phone.

Cell phones are the dominant way we access social media. Social media is a place where lust can become stimulated and run free. Scrolling on social media can stoke the lust for more money, power, and sex within both men and women. Also, too much social media can cause you to become jealous of what we perceive is happening in the lives of others. It can make us wish it were happening in our lives. Too much social media can feed the Dog and starve the Master. It can also make you feel discontent with your relationship, because you can find yourself inadvertently comparing it to those you see on social media.

For these reasons and many more, I highly recommend building a fence around phone and social media usage. Come up with suggestions that work for your relationship; for example, maybe no using the phone during the first two hours after getting home from work. Maybe no using the phone during dinner or no phone while you're watching TV together. This is too important to allow it to regulate itself. Work with your partner to set the right boundaries so you can protect your space and prevent Facebook, Instagram, Snapchat, YouTube, and Twitter from claiming your territory.

Regular Check-ins

Assumptions are major liabilities when dealing with the Dog and your relationship. Don't assume that just because you see each other regularly and you're spending time together, it automatically means you know how the other is really doing. Assumptions like these can do tremendous damage because your significant other could be struggling or suffering with something serious that has gone unspoken. Remember I said in the first chapter how the Dog likes to live in the shadows? Assumptions are one of the main things that keeps the shade down and the light away. Don't assume you or your significant other is doing okay. Ask.

Regular check-ins are important because they help keep a consistent flow of communication. We have to work on building and rebuilding communication because it's the lifeblood of a healthy relationship. A check-in is contact made to assess, acknowledge, or contribute to the well-being of your significant other. These can be formal or informal. Informal check-ins can look like texts throughout the day, and they can be simple: JUST

THINKING ABOUT YOU, HOPE YOUR DAY IS GOING GREAT, CAN'T WAIT TO SEE YOU TONIGHT, or HOW DID YOUR MEETING GO? Formal check-ins can mean actually scheduling a sit-down with each other, or going to see a therapist together, or going on a trip with the goal of reconnecting.

Women, the pressures on men are many and they are great. Pressures to succeed, provide, and live up to personal and private expectations can all produce a tremendous amount of stress. The Dog thrives in stressful situations because it can cause men to use the stress as justification to seek out remedies that are harmful (many of which I've already detailed). It's important to be sensitive to these pressures because the man in your life needs you more than he articulates. Just checking in regularly can do wonders for alleviating stress and helping calm the Dog. There have been times when I've had to tell Meagan, "I need you to check in on me more often, please don't assume that I'm okay. It may seem petty, but I need it." I had to own that it was my need and while she may not need the exact same thing from me, it's okay. Needs can and do differ. And thankfully, she has made the adjustment and it has helped me tremendously.

Men, don't allow your career pursuits to create such tunnel vision that you don't take the time to check on your woman. It's very important that even in the midst of the grind you let her know you're thinking about her and that you sincerely want to know how she's doing. Find out if there's anything you can take off her plate. Our careers can be so demanding that we can sometimes end up on autopilot and not be deliberate about making sure she is doing okay. Remember, women can stray too. When they don't feel valued or validated at home, it can make them vulnerable to getting their emotional needs met by another man because you've been so focused on achieving public success. Public success is important, but not when it comes at the expense of personal success. Taking care of your relationship is critical to becoming personally successful. Start checking in regularly. Put alarms in your phone to remind you and help you build the habit if you need to. Just a little consideration can go a long way and become an effective fence in your relationship.

Become an Expert at Meeting Each Other's Needs

Almost every year Meagan and I read Dr. Willard Harley's *His Needs, Her Needs: Building an Affair-Proof Marriage*. I highly recommend it as a tool to help you claim your territory in your relationship. One of the key tenets of the book is that great marriages are built on the goal of meeting each other's needs. As I've worked on meeting Meagan's needs in our marriage, I've definitely seen our bond become stronger. It's not enough to know what your significant other needs; you must also commit yourself to the process of becoming an expert at meeting those needs.

It sounds easy, yet it's one of the greatest challenges to remember that your needs may not be her needs, and vice versa. It's about learning to understand those needs and learning how your partner wants you to fulfill their needs. This is an awesome practice to help you master the Dog, because as we've discussed, the Dog is selfish. So when we as men commit ourselves to meeting the needs of our wives, it helps work against the Dog's selfish impulses. And a wife who is committed to meeting the needs of her husband can help keep the Dog in check and reduce the chances her husband will look outside the marriage to have those needs met.

Women, for so many reasons (some of which I'll cover in chapter 7) men are often reluctant to communicate or have trouble communicating freely with the woman in their life. If you find yourself in that situation, go ahead and make the first move toward better communication. Be open about your needs and emotions, and then invite your man to do the same. Let him know that not only will you not judge him for sharing how he feels, but you'll respect and love him even more for doing something he might find deeply uncomfortable. Once you've broken that barrier, stronger communication will be easier to create.

Schedule a marriage meeting with each other. Sit down and ask each other to list your top five needs. If you need help identifying what those needs are, check out *His Needs, Her Needs*. He lays out the top needs, from recreational companionship to sexual fulfillment. Once you identify your needs, ask each other how you would like those needs to be met. Put these needs in your phone so you can look at them frequently. Then go to work and become skilled at meeting these needs. I guarantee you will see your marriage go to another level when these needs are consistently met and fulfilled.

Build a Spiritual Fence

Just a look at the daily headlines will illustrate that as a society we're in trouble. Lust is winning. We're in dire straits, and immediate action is needed to reverse the trend. If you are a person of faith and wondering how spirituality can play a greater role in safeguarding your relationship, let me assure you that God and faith have a prominent place in this.

Men, as I said in chapter 3, rely on *The* Master. Pray and ask God for strength and He will make you stronger. God doesn't want men to act like dogs; He wants for us what we want for ourselves, which is to be the best men we can be. He wants us to have peace within our family and the love of a great woman. Isaiah 40:31 says: "Those who hope in the Lord will renew their strength. They will soar on wings like eagles; they will run and not grow weary, they will walk and not be faint" (NIV). If we ask God for strength of will, strength of mind, and strength of character, He will deliver it. Pray daily for strength, clarity of mind, and self-awareness and you'll find that you're better able to focus on stepping up as a partner, father, and leader. The serenity and inner peace you get from sharing personal time with the Lord will also help quiet the Dog and make it easier to command.

For women, your prayers are extremely effective in manifesting long-lasting protection and change in your relationship. If you have already tried, time and again, to make it work, but find that your relationship is still struggling, start or keep praying. Sometimes going vertical with a problem can help produce a solution that manifests vertically in our lives. My mother prayed for my alcoholic dad for years while he was strung out. Her prayer was that he would one day win the battle over addiction and return home to be the father and husband he wanted to be. God heard and answered her prayer and before he died, he came home clean and sober. As men, we can be so stubborn, yet your prayers can break through even when you feel like your words can't.

Here are some of the other supports specific to men that can help men protect their relationship:

Change Your Circle of Friends

In a piece for The Good Men Project, "Why I Cheated on All the Women I Loved," author and speaking coach Cliff Townsend writes with courage and candor about his life as a cheater and how he stopped cheating on the women in his life. In part of his confessional, he says:

> My mother had a saying when I was growing up . . . "If you lay down with stray dogs you will catch fleas." My translation was, "Son, you will become like the people you surround yourself with." All my friends cheated on their girlfriends and wives. My personal philosophy and my mind-set at the time made it acceptable for me to cheat. That was the reason I hung around with people who cheated. I wanted to be where my behavior was acceptable. . . . I was a cheater. I hung out with other cheaters.

We tend to hang with people who validate our behavior because they're doing the same things we are.

Men's interactions with other men powerfully affect ideas about what it means to be a man and how certain men choose to live up or down to that standard. Curating the tribe of men that you spend time with is an essential part of being the Master. This goes deeper than just watching who you hang out with. The goal isn't just to stop spending time with men who are living the way of the Dog but to spend more time with men who inspire you to live the way of the Master. Surrounding yourself with men who make you stronger and share your values means you're not dealing with the Dog alone. I probably wouldn't have the life I have today if not for the powerful men who, every day, remind me of my promises and my duty just by being who they are.

Surround yourself with men who are going in the same direction you are in life. Here's how you do it:

- **First, clean house.** Sever ties with men who have contributed to the behavior you're trying to avoid, or if you don't want to go that far, hang out with them less often.
- **Become more active in environments where you're likely to find men who put family, faith, and self-control first.** Your church, your work, a youth sports league, a community organization, or a nonprofit where you volunteer are good possibilities.
- **Be watchful.** Over time, the men in your tribe who genuinely want to be Masters and want the same for you will

show themselves. So will the players in a Master's clothing. When you figure out who's who, spend more time with the former and not so much with the latter.

Change Your Environment

Men, stop going to places that tempt you. Look at bars, clubs, parties, and other locations that get the Dog barking. What are the locations where you've failed the most often? Make it your business to find new ways to have fun and socialize that don't involve putting yourself in an environment that works against who you want to be.

Know Your Triggers

We talked about this in *The Wait*. There's no extra macho credit for staring temptation in the face and daring it to take you down. Why risk failure? Instead, be smart and avoid it altogether. Triggers are people, circumstances, or situations that weaken your ability to control the Dog. A trigger is anything that flips the lust switch in your brain and leads you to make reckless decisions.

Knowing your triggers can help you either avoid them or learn to overcome the impulses they spark. Know what makes you horny and what could set you in the wrong direction. If you still have phone numbers of exes in your phone and you're tempted by that, delete them. Avoid going to strip clubs. If you're on a date and you know going inside your date's house is going to become the point of no return, say goodbye at the door. If you're married and you know social media trips you up, put a limit on your daily scrolling time. Monitor the movies or TV shows you watch. Don't be naive about what can trip you up. Your triggers have power—respect that and plan accordingly.

Trips Can Be Traps

According to *The Normal Bar* by Chrisanna Northrup, Pepper Schwartz, and James Witte, thirty-six percent of men have cheated while on business trips. If business travel is an unavoidable part of your job as it is for mine, and you don't trust yourself completely, travel with a (male) counterpart or assistant. If your employer won't pay to have a second person accompany you, hire someone yourself who can serve as your virtual accountability person. Sure, it could get expensive to pay someone else to babysit you, but a divorce costs a lot more.

Find a Sponsor

Addicts have sponsors they can call when they're in immediate danger of relapsing; if you're worried that you can behave like an addict, you might need someone who can step in when you're in danger of letting the Dog take control. Make it someone who's committed to your welfare but stubborn enough not to listen to your excuses. Remember, your sponsor needs to be able to save you from yourself, and that might include going against your wishes in the moment. Give your sponsor permission to deliver tough love and accept it as a gift. I'll touch on this more in the "Create a Safe Space" chapter.

GO IN A NEW DIRECTION

You will never change your life until you change something
you do daily. The secret of your success is found in your daily
routine.

—JOHN C. MAXWELL

As we've discussed, Mastery takes a lifetime commitment. It bears repeating because for men to aspire to greatness, they must commit to the process of becoming great and work at it every single day. Bruce Lee was a master in martial arts. One of the reasons he became a master in this discipline was his lifetime commitment to Mastery.

He has two quotes that are my favorites. The first is: "I fear not the man who has practiced 10,000 kicks once, but I fear the man who has practiced one kick 10,000 times." The second is: "Art calls for complete mastery of techniques, developed by reflection within the soul." That's deep. Michelangelo, one of the immortals of art, said about Mastery, "No one has mastery, before he is at the end, of his art and his life." And the great Pablo Picasso said this about Mastery: "It took me a lifetime to paint like a child." When we commit to mastering ourselves, it's the work of a lifetime.

I wish there was some magic wand that would rid us of our lust forever, but there's not. This is our cross to bear. The Dog doesn't go away. So if we're going to be successful, we have to understand that Mastery is the goal not of a month or a year but a lifetime. Without that attitude, it's easy to find ourselves getting complacent or thinking we've got this thing beat and that's when men are most susceptible to the Dog.

Men, don't overestimate your strength. You can keep the Dog under tight control for years, but then you can become complacent, meet someone on a business trip or at the gym, and undo all your years of fidelity in one weak moment. The Master never underestimates the Dog or assumes he has completely tamed it.

Sometimes it feels like the Dog wants to break free and go crazy. That feeling can become aggressive, even dangerous, because you could become obsessed with figuring out how to satisfy the urge and this could make you feel incredibly weak for struggling to maintain control. Don't be alarmed. Feeling weak doesn't make you weak; it actually makes you stronger because you can admit your weakness. See how that works? When we admit that there are times we're not at our strongest, we empower ourselves to take steps to keep the Dog from getting loose and wrecking what we're doing.

That means we have to make plans. It also means we have to be smart. Think about Superman. In the comics and the movies he's the strongest man on the planet, but he knows that Kryptonite is his weakness. No matter how strong we are, we all have weaknesses and areas of vulnerability. So much of creating an effective barrier to keep the Dog confined is about avoiding temptation—not just resisting it but also not subjecting ourselves to it in the first place. Making plans to safeguard against temptation is essential to success.

That's sound strategy. If a man aspires to Mastery, he must invest time in cleaning up his life and clearing it of anything that gets the Dog worked up. One of the key things a man may need to do to claim the territory of a relationship is to change his routine.

On this topic, psychologist and certified sex addiction therapist Dr. Linda Hatch wrote in a blog post titled "Avoiding Temptation" for Psych Central, "Be aware of your ritual and change your routine. If you typically go to a certain store or coffee shop before you go home and binge on Internet porn, don't go to those places. If you get into prostitutes or hookups when you are on business trips, take precautions to do things that will change the pattern."

Changing his routine, aka "going in a new direction," really means changing everything about the pattern a man follows each day. The habits men follow on typical days when everything appears ordinary are the ones that shape who men ultimately become. Our daily habits become our life habits.

Men, try to sit down and write out the routines that structure your time for at least the five days of the workweek. For example:

• When and how you get to sleep
• Breakfast time

- Morning grooming routine
- Prayer, meditation, or affirmations
- Exercise regimen
- Diet throughout the day
- Work schedule
- Leisure time activities
- Intimate time with your partner
- Church time
- Time on the phone or on social media
- Work-related travel
- Answering email and phone calls

_____

_____

_____

_____

_____

_____

_____

_____

_____

_____

_____

_____

Once you map out your routine, evaluate where there are holes in it. Where are you losing time? Where are you lacking discipline? What could you do without and what do you need to do more of? You'd be surprised how seeing your current routine written down will help you assess the changes you need to make.

Living smarter means looking at every part of your daily routine with a critical eye and cleaning up the messy areas. If a man has been letting the Dog run his life, then it's time to change everything, and creating a new routine can help work wonders. How? Because a new routine breaks negative cycles that can keep us locked into perpetual patterns of bad behavior. My friend Jonathan McReynolds has a song called "Cycles," and one of the lyrics is "I'm not going in cycles, I'm gonna break these cycles." It's a powerful song that speaks to the necessity of changing routines in order to break free from dysfunctional cycles.

I've said it many times before and I'll say it again: discipline in the area of sex and romance leads to discipline and greater success in every other area of life. That's the premise of our book *The Wait*, and it's how I try to live my life. Many years ago when I decided to be celibate, I also decided I would adopt a deliberate, disciplined daily routine. I hoped that a new routine would change me into a man who would enjoy more success in all parts of his life.

I started doing CrossFit and working out twice a day. I became more mindful of what I ate. I began reciting a series of positive affirmations each morning. I took the time to invest in things like reading more screenplays to become better at my profession, doing speaking engagements, and engaging more with my faith. And today, the results of that, from my thriving career to the gift of my marriage to an incredible woman, are evident.

Routine is control. Control is power. It's possible to move through the world in a smarter way—planning, not reacting to what happens.

Write out a new routine. Get into a new groove. It's going to take time and repetition, but eventually the new habits will produce an almost spiritual rhythm that will create the foundation to reclaim any territory that has been lost or compromised.

The Couple That Plays Together Stays Together

Don't stop at finding a new routine; start one together. Do something fun with your significant other. This is an often overlooked but effective way of protecting your yard. Having shared interests keeps the relationship fresh and aligned. Work out together, go to church together, take up a new hobby together—find things you like to do together and build them into your life. The more you spend time doing things you both enjoy, the closer you will become and the stronger your bond will become. It's very hard to violate a yard that's well protected, and playing together has the wonderful effect of creating a yard that neither of you will ever want to leave.

CHAPTER 6

DISCIPLINE THE DOG

*We must all suffer one of two things: the pain of discipline or
the pain of regret.*
—JIM ROHN, AMERICAN BUSINESS PHILOSOPHER

My habits protect my life but they would assassinate you.
—MARK TWAIN, AMERICAN AUTHOR

Once upon a time, years ago, I was dating a great woman.
After a while, she and I broke up but remained friends.
Then I started dating someone new, but I neglected to tell her
I was seeing someone else. I don't know what I was thinking.
Was I keeping her in the dark because I wanted to have her as
a backup in case my new relationship didn't work out? Was I
too scared to man up and tell her and risk hurting her feelings?
I don't know, maybe both answers are true. All I know is that
I didn't have much discipline in my dating life and it almost
came back to bite me in a big way.

One night my ex called me. She had just flown back into
town and had a gift she wanted to give me on her way home

from Los Angeles International Airport. I wasn't strong enough to tell her, "No, don't come over," even though the girl I was currently dating would be arriving at my place at around the same time. So I told her, "Okay, but only for a moment." She said, "Cool." A few minutes went by, and I was sweating. *What have I done?* Then, the sound of the doorbell made my heart skip a beat.

It was my ex. I invited her in, gave her a hug, but didn't invite her to sit down and didn't sit myself. I took the gift, opened it, and said, "Thank you so much. You know, I really appreciate this. You didn't have to do this." While I was speaking, I was walking her to the back door of my apartment. We hugged again, and then I said, "Thank you so much. I appreciate you. I'll call you." And I ushered her out the door, hoping my act hadn't raised her suspicions.

By the time I walked back into my apartment the doorbell was ringing again. It was the girl I was dating, excited and ready for a night out. The two women had missed each other—and I had dodged an uncomfortable, potentially explosive, scene—by maybe thirty seconds. It was like something out of a sitcom, except for the part where I was sweating and my heart was racing.

In the moment, I was grateful I wasn't found out. But as trivial as this story may be to some, what it revealed in me was something far more serious: a lack of discipline.

SELF-CONTROL IS EVERYTHING

When it comes to dog training, discipline means punishment, but that wasn't the kind of discipline I realized I was lacking. My lack of discipline revealed a lack of self-control. Self-control is a problem for men when it comes to lust. There is research that confirms we all have something in common with dogs. According to Stephanie Pappas, "Both [us and dogs] get worn out having to exert self-control and end up making dumb decisions, a new study finds." Holly Miller of the University of Lille Nord de France says, "When humans are depleted, they are less helpful, more aggressive, gamble more, etc. . . . these consequences also have biological roots. When dogs are depleted, they too are more likely to behave rashly and impulsively."

In my experience, self-control is one of the main areas the Dog attacks. Lustful desires demand to be fed. Yet the demand isn't the issue; the issue is men's inability or unwillingness to resist the demand. The difficulty in resistance is a result of two issues, and the one compounds the other. As I've mentioned, men's lust gets fed and enticed often, so over time the persistence of lustful messages can wear down the resistance of even the strongest men. The stresses and pressures of the constant pursuit of goals, ambitions, and career progress compound this. The stress can be so intense that the ability to resist the power of lust can, at times, seem futile because the fulfillment of that particular lustful desire can feel like a way to cope with the stress. But understanding this doesn't excuse the need for self-control.

Empowering the Master to help in this area is critical if a man is ever going to win the battle.

Men, if you think your professional drive and achievements can keep you insulated from the liability of lacking self-control, you are grossly mistaken. As I've noted, professional success and personal success are different. Any lack of self-control poses a threat to us both personally and professionally. When we overlook a major personal deficiency like lack of self-control, over time it ultimately comes to disrupt any professional success we may have. This is why we've got to do the work on getting more self-control.

Women, you can learn a lot about a man based on his level of self-control or lack thereof. Self-control is the foundation of discipline, and discipline is the foundation of every attempt at Mastery. Sometimes it can be tempting to look beyond the negative you see in a man because it doesn't line up with the ideal of what you want to see. Resist this temptation. Be honest and open about what you see so you can empower yourself to navigate the situation accordingly. This goes for both romantic and professional situations. There are some men you may deal with who don't exhibit much self-control and haven't yet committed to doing the work. What does this look like? In a romantic sense, it could look like a man who always wants recreation more than dedication, who insists on always having his way, who never wants to engage in meaningful conversation, who slacks off in his work and doesn't really see any one thing in his life all the way through. Professionally, it could take the form of a man making inappropriate comments or lewd gestures, engaging in misogynistic behavior, or even expressing sexist views. From a romantic standpoint, understanding this can help you decide how you want to deal with the situation. If you're dating a man who doesn't have self-control, you have the power to decide if it's worth it to keep going or if you're going to bring this to his attention and see if he's willing to make changes. If you're married to a man and you notice he lacks self-control, bring it to his attention and commit to working through it with him. In a professional setting, recognizing you work with a man who lacks self-control might help you avoid uncomfortable situations with him.

SACRIFICE IS THE KEY

I want to go back to my near miss for a moment. When I began to review my decisions and the steps that led me to that near miss, I realized my pattern revealed a lack of discipline. If I had been more disciplined at that time, I would have been more upfront with my ex and not led her on in any way. But secretly, truth be told, I kind of wanted to have my cake and eat it too.

At the time I was an executive for Sony, flying all around the world, making hit films—a life that, for some, would be a sign of tremendous success. However, when we judge someone outwardly as a success without any knowledge of what they do personally, it's the equivalent of going on the Studio Tour at Universal and admiring the beautiful houses on the back lot. Once you see them from the back, you realize they are all a facade, with nothing behind the attractive surface. Having limited discipline in my private life yet maintaining a facade of discipline in my professional/public life made me no different from the houses on that back lot. This is why I believe whole-heartedly:

No Discipline = No Destiny

Discipline unlocks potential. In order for us (both men and women) to be who we were created to be, discipline is and always will be an essential ingredient. To achieve the greatest this life has to offer, we (especially men) must employ rigorous discipline in every area of life. What is discipline? *Discipline* means harnessing the unified power of the mind, body, and spirit through self-control and sacrifice.

Discipline and desire go hand in hand. Whatever you desire, that's where you must discipline yourself the most. And sacrifice always accompanies discipline.

- What are you willing to go without to get what you want?
- What are you willing to sacrifice to achieve your goals?

It is very difficult to harness the power of discipline in these three areas (mind, body, spirit) all at once when no sacrifice is present. *Sacrifice* means going without something you want in the present in order to achieve something greater in the future.

Think about it. When you're on a diet you're trying to exert discipline over your appetite by going without certain foods in the moment for the greater goal of achieving the physical look or health you desire. It's painful to not eat foods you really enjoy, but if you want to lose weight or get healthier more than you want to keep eating food that makes you unhealthy, you give up (sacrifice) the food that prevents you from achieving the future you want. This is no easy task; sacrifice is painful.

Discipline, sacrifice, self-control, and desire all work together—and that's where some of the trouble surfaces.

OUR DESIRES ARE AT WAR

No discipline seems pleasant at the time, but painful. Later on, however, it produces a harvest of righteousness and peace for those who have been trained by it.

—HEBREWS 12:11 (NIV)

Our desires are at war with themselves. We desire to go to bed early to get a head start on the next day, yet we also desire to stay up a little later to finish binge-watching our favorite show. We desire to save money to buy a new car, yet we also desire to buy a new pair of shoes that just came out. We desire to get ahead on the job, yet we also desire to maintain the status quo. Every single day we are engaged in a war between our differing desires and have to choose which desire will win out. The desire for immediate pleasure, aka gratification, is so strong that it can disrupt the desire for discipline.

Of course, all of us, both men and women, have a need for pleasure. I'm not saying that all pleasure is wrong; of course it's not. However, when not tempered by discipline the pursuit of pleasures leads to destructive decision-making. For example, going back to the dieting analogy, if you automatically eat whatever you want every time you're hungry, what happens? In the moment, you might experience great pleasure because the hunger pangs are satisfied by tasty food. However, that will become destructive in the long run because of the toll this type of eating takes on your long-term health (obesity, diabetes, high blood pressure, etc.). Men giving in to the desires of the Dog create a similar dynamic.

The Dog wants to consume as much pleasure as possible while avoiding the sacrifice that discipline brings. The Dog wants men to react in the moment and satisfy every urge without thinking about what happens when the moment is over. When men do this consistently, it creates a self-centered motivation wherein they are primarily focused on fulfilling their needs, wants, and desires above all else. This can create a moral blind spot where they become so fixated on satisfying the desire for immediate pleasure that they become oblivious to the negative behavior this type of focus creates.

This is one of the reasons things in our society have gotten so out of control—because men's desire for immediate, self-centered, lustful pleasure has taken priority over everything else. The constant feeding of the Dog and the avoidance of discipline and sacrifice have led men to follow their lowest instincts and nature over and over again.

Change starts with incorporating a consistent diet of discipline into your daily life. Discipline is the key to health, true wealth, and total well-being. However, the Dog wants nothing to do with this, and it hates the sacrifice and pain that come with delayed gratification. Remember, it wants what it wants when it wants it. However, a certain level of pain is part of a well-disciplined life, and this is the good type of pain that will produce unprecedented positive results in life. It is painful to forgo eating a piece of cake when we really want it, but when we do this consistently, the results we experience when we look in the mirror are worth the pain. Psychotherapist Dr. Ilene S. Cohen says this about the avoidance of pain:

> [W]hat happens when you want to be instantly satisfied in all areas of your life? What happens when you only avoid pain? . . . Living for a purpose becomes impossible at that point, because a life spent avoiding pain doesn't result in goals getting accomplished. . . . When we live in pursuit of immediate pleasure—needing to have the newest gadget . . . wanting the perfect job without getting an education or working our way up from the bottom—we become just like toddlers again, completely incapable of delaying gratification.

The solution is *discipline*. Discipline is the key. Discipline means we can't do whatever we want whenever we want. What I know for sure is that:

*Discipline unlocks the potential in a man. When a man ap-
plies discipline to his life, there's nothing he can't do.*

WILL POWER

Take Will Smith. He's been my mentor and friend for more than twenty years, and he is a master of self-discipline. How else do you think he became one of the biggest movie stars in the world, a successful producer and businessman, a devoted husband, and a globally respected figure? Not by accident. He has achieved all this through self-control and discipline.

It's not just talent. Will has loads of talent, but he'll be the first to tell you that it's not his talent alone that got him this far. It's not just hard work alone, because there are many actors who work hard. The key to Will's accomplishments is the powerful combination of talent, hard work, and self-discipline. He uses discipline to harness the Master within to become the best man he can be.

Will started an Instagram account in 2017 and has been using it to motivate the masses. I love it because he's now giving the world the same knowledge he's been providing me privately for years. He did a series of videos on the central role self-discipline plays in getting what you want. In them he points out (correctly) that ninety-nine percent of people with big dreams won't do the work necessary to make those dreams happen. Because it's *hard*.

"At the center of bringing any dream into fruition," he says, "is self-discipline." He goes deep when he insists that discipline is about getting command of your mind so you can choose actions that are in your best interest. Instead, every day, he says, we make choices that aren't in our best interest.

Why? Because we, especially men, let our urges and impulses drive us without stopping to think before we act. How many times have you decided you were sick of being out of shape, broke, or tired of living beneath your potential and vowed to change your ways? And how many times have you lasted for a little while but ended up going right back to the poor choices that were making you dissatisfied in the first place?

Our life becomes the sum total of the decisions we make. When we consistently make decisions that favor our best interests, over time we position our life to begin to reflect the character of those decisions.

Who we want to be and what we want to accomplish all starts in our mind, so we have to have the will to become the best we can be in this life, then use discipline to achieve it.

DISCIPLINE 101

Putting dogs through obedience training requires tremendous discipline on the part of the owner. When the dog owner is inconsistent and lacks discipline, the dog will become a mirror and begin to exhibit the same inconsistency and lack of discipline. This is why every dog owner who wants to become the master of their dog must commit to training their dog consistently, even when they don't feel like it.

We've all had moments when we sabotaged our progress by not staying committed to discipline. When it comes to men, disciplining the Dog starts with the decision to take control and make the Dog obedient. Becoming disciplined is about practicing delayed gratification by replacing negative choices and habits with choices and habits that feed the Master. Men, here are some suggestions for achieving discipline. Ladies, much of this advice can apply to your life as well, so read on.

Start Sacrificing Now

Sacrificing is a form of delayed gratification. Reject pleasures that derail long-term goals. Remember to make choices that are in your best interest. Sorry to be a buzzkill, but discipline starts with self-denial. If you want to become your best, quit eating a diet of vice. As we've discussed, empty pleasures that only satisfy lust are Dog food, and the more the Dog is fed, the stronger it gets. But don't think of this process as simply about giving things up.

Sacrificing also makes room for choices and habits that will bring you happiness and peace. The ancient Greek philosopher Aristotle said: "True happiness comes from gaining insight and growing into your best possible self. Otherwise all you're having is immediate gratification pleasure, which is fleeting and doesn't grow you as a person." Dr. Cohen says this about delayed gratification: "Whether it's saving for that future dream house, choosing a healthy lifestyle now to stay healthy as you age, or putting up with a difficult job to help boost your career for the long term, delayed gratification can yield tremendous returns while helping you develop a tolerance for waiting."

Here are some practical examples of how to activate sacrifice:

- Instead of going straight home after work, go to the gym and work out. Your body is the temple of God, but if you don't take care of it, it can start to crumble.
- Instead of eating that bagel and orange juice in the morning (over fifty grams of carbs!), choose wisely what you put into your body and go for the oatmeal and water.
- Instead of staying up late watching your favorite TV show, go to bed. Waking up early works wonders for your productivity.
- For men, instead of dating multiple women, commit to dating just one.
- For men, instead of spending time working so much, spend more time with your wife or girlfriend.

- Instead of just hoping for career advancement, go back to school and get your degree or advanced degree.
- Instead of just spending time being consumed with your own affairs, take some time to volunteer in the community.
- Instead of just watching service online, go back to church.
- Instead of sleeping in, get up early to pray and meditate.
- Instead of doing just enough to get by, step up to take on more responsibility at work.
- Instead of just scrolling and reading articles on Facebook, read books to feed your mind.
- Instead of just watching sports, spend more time planning for the future.
- Instead of spending all your money on clothes, start saving money deliberately.

You get the picture. When you activate sacrifice, you build discipline.

Make New Habits

As I've said before, I have a daily routine that's done nothing but enhance my success in every area of my life. After I wake up, I pray, recite positive affirmations, and read the Bible. I work out nearly every day, and sometimes twice a day. I do a green, plant-based protein shake every day (I even travel with the ingredients so I can make it when I'm on the road). I observe the Sabbath. Every Friday at sunset, I set my work aside (not an easy thing to do in the movie business) and turn off my social media and email until sunset the next day. During this time I pray, study the Bible, preach, and spend time in fellowship with my family. It's like taking a deep, cleansing breath. When the Sabbath is over, I turn my phone back on, watch it come back to life with texts and emails, and jump back into work.

I'm strict about my routine for good reason. I found that when I put more discipline into my daily schedule, that same discipline became a force for good in every other area of my life. It has made every other part of my life, from my career to my personal relationships, richer and deeper. A lot of the improvement was spiritual. As I used great discipline and discovered the Master inside me, I started applying the same principles to my work, health, and friendships.

I activated sacrifice. I adopted positive behaviors and repeated them until they became habits. I surrounded myself with people of integrity and character. I was able to work longer hours and produce better work. I was fitter and had more energy. I started to build stronger relationships with people across a wide array of industries, relationships based on mutual trust and respect. Over a period of a few years, everything came together in my life.

After a man has started to activate sacrifice and set a goal that's more important to him than the fleeting pleasures of sex, money, or power, the next essential component of discipline is creating a routine that works and practicing it continuously. He then has to stick to it until it becomes normal. As discussed in the "Go in a New Direction" section in the previous chapter, routines are habits for positive change.

There are many ways to make new habits, and the more automatic you make your schedule, the more the discipline will become a pleasurable habit rather than a dreaded chore. Find a routine that works for you, hit Start, and repeat, day after day, month after month. As with working out, don't worry about seeing results from day to day. Just put your head down and stick to the routine. If something isn't working, make an adjustment. But keep doing the work. The results will come.

Start Discipline Now (Especially if You're Single)

For men, become disciplined now, especially if you're single. Remember the crucial point I made in *The Wait*: *A man who is not disciplined in his dating life will have a hard time being disciplined in his marriage.* But if a man starts practicing discipline in his dating life, this will translate into discipline in a committed relationship, and then discipline in marriage.

When a man gets married, he's officially saying that he wants the Master within to be in control. He makes a promise and a vow to the woman in his life. However, if that man hasn't practiced discipline before getting married, then the Dog in him will be well fed while the Master is malnourished as he stands at the altar. When the euphoria of marriage subsides, who will be in a better position to have the most control in his life? The Dog.

Years before I met Meagan, I made a decision to exercise discipline over my sexual life because I was leading a double life: preaching about monogamy but not living it in my personal life. I didn't want to be a hypocrite. As I started the process of waiting until marriage to have sex again, I began to discover the power of activating sacrifice. This was helpful because once I got married I realized the benefit of having laid a solid foundation of discipline while I was dating. It gave me a strong foundation of discipline in my marriage. I already had practice managing my urges, controlling my behavior, and keeping the Dog in check.

Discipline in a man's dating life leads not only to discipline in his marriage but also to discipline in every other aspect of his life. Discipline is contagious, and the more it's practiced, the more success will be found in all areas of life. Discipline will help improve health, career, fitness, finances—everything. Becoming disciplined in dating will spill over in the best way.

However, I want to be clear about something: There's nothing magical about marriage vows. They don't turn a player into a faithful husband and didn't magically turn me into one, either. It takes work every single day and a firm, unwavering commitment to being the man I want to be.

Why does it seem like it's so hard for a man to keep his vows? It's not because a man doesn't *intend* to keep his vows when he gets married. It's because when he's a single guy who's sleeping with every woman he sees, he's living an undisciplined life.

After he gets married, it becomes difficult to live a life of discipline if he hasn't had practice living that way until that point. Most men struggle with fidelity, but without sexual discipline in dating, that struggle gets amplified and makes it very difficult for even men with the best intentions to stay committed to those marriage vows.

If you are a married man and didn't practice this type of discipline while you were dating, don't worry—hope is not lost. Use the advice and tips I've given in this book. You can be faithful and committed if you desire to be. Marriage in and of itself doesn't tame the Dog. Discipline tames the Dog by making you the Master. The Master in you will respond if you commit to the process of becoming the man you were created to be through discipline and sacrifice.

Also, I must address the question of "Are we created to be monogamous?" Because there are some men that deep down don't believe we were created to be monogamous and as a result they can use this as justification to cheat. I believe we were created with the capacity and disposition for monogamy, however, I know there are many differing points of view on this subject. Yet, the answer isn't found in the question; the answer is found in our choice. We have the power to choose and when we pick monogamy we possess the ability to adapt our lifestyle and behavior accordingly.

CURB YOUR DOG

"Curb your dog" is a phrase that encourages dog owners to clean up after their dogs. There are some states that will fine dog owners if they don't do so. When a dog makes a mess, it's the owner's responsibility to clean it up. There's nothing worse than going to the park or walking on the sidewalk and stepping in a dog's mess because the owner didn't take care of their responsibility. This is why there are fines for those who shirk their responsibility; the fines keep dog owners accountable.

Accountability is essential to discipline.

One of the big reasons sexual harassment has become such a plague in society is the lack of accountability. For much too long men have gotten by on the credit card of "just being men." Men have gotten away with despicable behavior because some men haven't been held accountable—and sometimes refused to hear the women who were the victims, or even blamed them. Now the bill for all this is coming due. Change can start when men accept the mantle of accountability and allow others to hold them accountable.

The Dog hates accountability because it doesn't want consequences like remorse and punishment. But the Master welcomes accountability, because he knows being held to a higher standard makes him better in the long run, and that's his focus. He doesn't mind being called on the carpet for negative behavior, because he knows the rebuke is a reminder that he's better than that.

Men, we must hold *ourselves* accountable. As I've said before, when we see something, we must say something. We must value being good men above all else. We must choose not to become unfaithful because we love our women, value our marriages, and don't ever want to cause devastation and pain. I want us to start appreciating our women, our calling, our creation, and ourselves more highly. I want us to see ourselves as healers, leaders, protectors, fathers, and husbands. If we see the value in these qualities and know that it's them—not sex—that make us men, it sets a standard by which we can hold ourselves accountable for being the kind of men we aspire to be.

Respect is a critical part of accountability. Dogs don't respect boundaries. They'll sniff around someone else's garbage and dig holes in the neighbor's yard. It's the same for the Dog. It does whatever it takes to get what it wants: lie, cheat, manipulate, flatter, you name it. But for a Master, discipline is a show of respect for himself and everyone he holds dear.

As men, we want to be respected, but respect is earned. If you want respect from the woman you're with, show her respect first. Be honest on dates. Show concern for her needs and regard for her ambitions. Trust her when you're not together. Be proud of her strength and independence instead of being intimidated by them. And don't make being with her all about sex. If you reject a woman just because she won't sleep with you, you might turn away what could be the best thing to happen to you.

A woman who is not willing to go to bed with a man at his request is a sign of a good woman, not the other way around.

Perhaps most important of all, if your woman holds you accountable when you fail at discipline, accept that as a sign of respect. A woman will hold you accountable if she believes in you and in who you really are (even if your actions don't always show it).

Women, don't be afraid to hold your man accountable for his actions, especially those actions that come from the Dog. Truth be told, the Dog responds most to pain. If you fail at holding him accountable because you're afraid of losing him or you're afraid of how he'll respond, you're doing him and yourself a disservice. If the man you're with consistently exhibits a pattern of behavior that is disruptive, sometimes pain is the only thing that will make him decide to change. Now I'm not talking about physical pain. I'm talking about the pain of potentially losing you. Your request for accountability might be a source of great pain to him. How? Because that accountability might take the form of breaking up for a while or expressing the desire to separate from him while he gets the help he needs. Holding someone else accountable isn't easy, yet it's necessary for a healthy relationship.

Ladies, here's an important sidenote: don't let your desire for accountability turn into nitpicking. Holding your man accountable means being rational, clear, calm, and focused on what your man needs to do to make things right. Nitpicking is when you find fault with every action, and instead of using discretion about which things to voice, you voice everything, and that has the potential to damage your relationship. Trust me, if he's a decent guy, he's already punishing himself for any time he's missed the mark with you. If there are areas where he needs accountability, tell him calmly, firmly, and with love what he needs to do to make things right. Then give him time to right his wrongs.

PRACTICE MAKES PERFECT

Discipline is hard even when it becomes a habit. But if you practice discipline long enough, you'll develop integrity. That's the key word: *practice*. A practice is something we work at daily. In terms of the Dog, this means never losing sight of what the Dog is, what it wants, and what it'll do to get it. It means never letting your guard down and understanding the consequences of doing so.

For men, the practice of discipline starts with the aspiration to be the Master. To start developing your own discipline practice, try asking yourself some challenging questions:

- What do I want badly enough to practice strict self-discipline?

- What will be the damage—emotional, financial, reputational—if I fail?

- Am I ready to be held accountable for my behavior?

- If I'm single, how do I attract good women into my life?

- How can I earn the respect of others?

- How can I have less drama and conflict in my life?

- What does the woman in my life deserve from me?

- Can I be a role model to other men?

- How can I make amends to anyone the Dog in me has hurt?

Your answers will help you know where to begin practicing. Building sustainable habits will help you navigate those moments when you're weak because you'll already have a pattern of healthy habits and proven tools to rely on.

For women, here are some questions to ask yourself:

- How much discipline do I have in all areas of my life?

- Am I asking the man in my life to be more disciplined when I'm not that disciplined myself?

- Am I allowing negative behavior from an undisciplined man in my life?

- How do I need to be better supported in my relationship?

- How can I have less drama and conflict in my life?

- Am I getting what I truly deserve in life?

- How can I model discipline more consistently?

- How can I use discipline to heal from the wounds of my past?

Let's look at some methods that will help men establish the practice of discipline:

Remind yourself what you have to lose. Thanks to the smartphone, a man can have photos, audio recordings, and videos of his wife, children, or significant other with him 24/7. I know men who look at photos of their families when they're tempted by another woman. This helps remind them how much they have to lose. If he's a good man, the idea of hurting and losing the respect of those he loves will tear him up inside. He must use that to his advantage and to keep himself strong.

Eliminate anything that lowers inhibitions. How many times have you heard about a guy who cheated on his wife or girlfriend because he got drunk? How many times have you done something you regret when you've had a few too many? Lay off the alcohol, weed, or any other mind-altering substance, period. Any substance that lowers inhibitions and impairs judgment makes it easier for the Dog to get off the leash.

Talk to someone. In the next chapter I will discuss how it helps to have a safe space where men can be open about their struggles with the Dog, get encouragement, and know that they aren't alone. A man may also need to talk with a therapist, counselor, or doctor—this isn't to be feared. There is no shame in getting whatever help is needed.

Be honest with yourself about your motivation. When a man is considering doing something being fueled by lust, it's important to do a motivation check. A man should ask himself, "Am I looking at hiring her not because she's the best candidate for the job but because she's the best looking?" or "Am I thinking about going to that movie not because I care about seeing it but because my girlfriend's gorgeous sister is going?" Making choices fueled by lust is detrimental to the man *and* to whoever is on the receiving end of these decisions. It's also a potential danger zone for cheating or harassment. Motivations must constantly be checked and rechecked.

Stop using the Dog as an excuse to manipulate situations or get women to do what you want them to do. If a man is being manipulative, he risks letting the Dog off the leash and sabotaging the very discipline he's trying to achieve. Men shouldn't date with sex as the primary objective. When men do this it causes them to potentially reject great woman, to their detriment.

STOP THE SEX

Finally, I can't talk about men and discipline without talking about sex. For single men, have you ever considered being celibate?

Now, before you throw the book across the room, stay with me. I know this isn't an easy choice. If it were, I wouldn't hear from women all the time who are incredibly frustrated because they can't find good men who are willing to wait for sex, even for a short time. But if a man is trying to master the Dog and change his life, shouldn't celibacy be on the list of ways to do so?

Think about it in terms of changing your diet. For some men making small changes to what they eat doesn't work because they only respond to extreme changes. So they try intermittent fasting or even total fasting to jump-start weight loss and improvements in their health. Waiting for sex is the same thing—when a man gives up sex, it can be the jump start his life needs.

If that seems like too much to ask, consider this. Look at the collateral damage of an undisciplined sex life. If a man has rejected or hurt good women because he couldn't get sex from them, or if he has chosen someone just because she would sleep with him and wound up in a dysfunctional situation, how could celibacy be worse? Speaking from experience, it's not.

I challenge any single man reading this to try celibacy for at least a month and note the positive changes you experience when your life isn't based around how, when, and with whom you're going to have sex. Stopping sex until marriage can unleash a power you've never experienced before and propel you to personal and professional heights you've never reached. It will clear your mind, enhance your focus, and allow you time to heal. You may not realize it, but all the women you've slept with have taken an emotional toll on your spirit because they kept the Dog hungry long after you got out of bed with them. I know so many men who have almost lost the ability to commit to a woman because so many sexual encounters have corrupted their spirit to the degree where nothing or no one can ever be good enough. It's okay to stop. It's okay to not allow your sexual prowess to corrupt your manhood. It's okay to say no. It's okay to wait.

Celibacy is the ultimate self-discipline. As I said before: if you can get discipline in your sexual life, there's nothing you can't do.

CHAPTER 7

CREATE A SAFE SPACE

A lot of these are guys coming from a tumultuous life,
including myself. Some people need outlets, a way to express
yourself.

—KEVIN HART, COMEDIAN

Men are taught, point-by-point, not to feel, not to cry, and not
to find words to express themselves.

—DAPHNE ROSE KINGMA, AUTHOR OF *THE MEN WE NEVER KNEW*

A dog has a constant need to feel safe, and when that safety isn't readily available a myriad of behavioral issues can occur. This safety is best experienced in what dog trainers call a safe space. Dog expert Sarah Wilson writes, "Right now, if you have a dog with separation issues, you are probably his safe place. . . . [W]hen you walk out the door, his safety goes with you. So our task is to create a safe place in your home that is always there when he needs it." A safe space is necessary to give a dog a feeling of stability and peace.

Dr. Jennifer Cattet is a doctor of ethology (animal behavior) and cofounder of Medical Mutts. Medical Mutts is a company that focuses on helping those who need service dogs and helping dogs that have been abandoned. She writes, "Barking, aggression, destruction, separation anxiety . . . [m]any behavior issues that directly affect the dog's welfare can be attributed to stress and fear. . . . Just like in humans, many attribute aggressive displays as signs of strength and character. In reality they're an expression of underlying feelings of being threatened. . . . When animals are anxious or afraid, their number one priority is to feel safe again."

In all the research I've done for this book, the concept of a safe space was one of the ideas that resonated most deeply with me. A safe space is something men desperately need because so many men, including myself at times, suffer in silence. Men, for the most part, don't know how to talk about what's really going on in their lives, and don't have the language or ability to communicate it in any case. Women, I'm going to go deep in this chapter to give you a better understanding of the real truth about men.

These are the secret questions that persist inside a man:

- Where do I go when I can't tell anyone how I feel?
- Who do I talk to when the Dog starts raging and I'm afraid to admit I'm not as righteous as I portray myself to be?
- How do I learn to love someone else when I'm not even sure I love myself?

- When is it okay to confess that I am struggling with lust when I know I can't say anything to my significant other because it will freak her out?

The battle with lust can be intense, and sometimes it can feel like men are flat-out losing. What makes it even worse is that men are conditioned *not* to talk about feelings. Men are taught that it's weak to express them. Men don't know whom they can talk to without being judged. As a result, the feelings most men experience get compounded because there doesn't seem to be anywhere to go.

Men are told to be tough and "suck it up." Men don't always have the permission to express their feelings; in most circumstances, it's not allowed. Sometimes that makes them come off as non-communicative. But communicated or not, the feelings are there—the doubt, the fear, the longing, the loneliness, the regret. So men suffer in silence. I can't tell you how many men I know who have experienced this. As I've mentioned, I've been in the church all my life, but not even in the church do men find complete refuge.

Because of this, men feel compelled to present the image that we've got it all together. "It's all good. *Worry? Doubt? Not me.*" There's a fear that if men express anything to the contrary, especially when it comes to dealing with lust, they will be ridiculed, shamed, or worse.

That silence is killing men. According to the American Foundation for Suicide Prevention, not only is suicide the tenth leading cause of death in the United States, but men in the U.S. commit suicide three-and-a-half times more often than women. Psychology professor Cheryl Meyer of Wright State University says "hegemonic masculinity" is killing men because they are trying to live up to a social stereotype that absolutely no man can measure up to. In an article for *Big Think* by Philip Perry, Meyer describes hegemonic masculinity as the idea that "[a man's] machismo must be broadcast constantly, no matter what he is dealing with or how he feels inside. It's stoicism taken to the nth degree." Several studies have found that hegemonic masculinity is detrimental to men's well-being and overall health. For far too long, men have clung to this false standard of what it means to be a "real man."

Men are at their best when experiencing and expressing honestly. But most of us are robbed of that; when we don't conform to societal norms we are met with rejection and ridicule. It can be painful to open up about what we think, fear, and care about. My good friend, Grammy Award winner Israel Houghton, said in an Instagram post, "If I'm actually honest with people, I run a high risk of being rejected. If people actually knew who I really was and what I'm really grappling with and what I'm really struggling with . . . I don't want to be honest with people because I've seen what happens to people who are honest . . . they get ostracized, they get isolated, they get marginalized, they get talked about. And so you find yourself holding on as tight as you can to the persona, to the platform, to the reputation."

As we've discussed, one of the reasons so many men turn to vice is because it provides immediate relief for the stress they feel while trying to keep up the appearance that everything's okay. Without a healthy outlet to help them process the battle with lust, it's tempting to retreat to unhealthy habits and detrimental immediate pleasures (gambling, drinking, womanizing, cheating, pornography, etc.) just to feel better for a little while. The Dog works overtime; it doesn't take breaks. It's easy for men to feel trapped and powerless—pressured to keep up the image that wins approval while simultaneously trying to live virtuously. It's exhausting, and nobody seems to understand or care what many men are going through. When men have no appropriate place to let that pressure out, there's a tendency to just throw up our hands and say, "What the hell!" Vice becomes a drug that eases the pain.

That's a slippery slope down to becoming the men we don't want to be. Creating a safe space is the solution.

THE SAFE SPACE

> Man's inability to communicate is a result
> of his failure to listen effectively.
> —CARL ROGERS, PSYCHOLOGIST

Growing up without a father, I had a lot of anger in me—anger at my dad for not being around, anger at him for cheating on my mother, anger at being the middle child, and anger at the world in general. My anger might have changed who I became as an adult if not for the Oakland Men's Project (OMP), one of the leading organizations at the time in dealing with the root cause of men's violence. I started taking conflict resolution and violence management training classes through the OMP as part of a high school leadership program, and was blessed with the company of wise men who trained me in how to deal with my anger—training that laid the groundwork for mastering the Dog later in life.

The Oakland Men's Project was started by Paul Kivel and Allan Creighton and program director Heru-Nefara Amen, and was created to help prevent male violence against men and women. They did incredible work with me, as well as a generation of young men and women in the Bay Area. Their patient, insightful teaching helped us clearly see, for the first time, how most men have been conditioned to respond to the challenges of the world with some form of rage and violence.

At the OMP, I learned the ways that men, when denied healthy ways of expressing fear or doubt, exert control over others through harsh words, anger, intimidation, and, sometimes, physical violence. I also saw how so much of the conflict that leads men to become damaged occurs not just through large-scale violence but through smaller, subtler acts of violence: yelling, undermining comments, and insults, such as being called stupid, worthless, or weak.

I learned firsthand what men are capable of becoming when they don't have a healthy environment to express who they really are. Through the OMP's teachings, I also learned that being a man meant controlling the anger that had filled me since my father's death and steering myself toward compassion, service, and faith. It was my first true experience with a safe space.

A safe space is the antidote to the destructive and all-too-common stereotype of what it means to be a man—the idea that says it's not okay for men to be vulnerable, show our feelings, talk about our troubles, fail, or cry.

A safe space is an environment where men can express themselves honestly without fear of judgment or punishment.

Men need a space—and this doesn't always mean a physical space—to talk to other men (and certain women; more on this later) about the challenges of dealing with lust, pressures, fears, and anxieties, and discuss what must be done to maintain control and become better men. They need a supportive environment where they can deal with feelings of shame, guilt, anger, frustration, and vulnerability. Men need a safe place to swap stories, share ideas and strategies, pray together, and feel understood.

You see, most men want to be better. Men don't want to feel helpless when it comes to controlling the Dog. Men don't want to ruin their lives, cause pain to the women they love, or damage their reputation and integrity. Men aren't helpless, but men do need help, and it's not women's responsibility to provide it. It's men's responsibility to help each other tap into the love within. A safe space is a place of empathy and support where men can pursue the love within, knowing that when they stumble, there will be accountability but not judgment.

Traditionally, men haven't had a place like this, a place where it's safe to open up and be vulnerable. Our manhood culture is built on the idea that to be vulnerable is to be less of a man. It's just not true. True manhood is found in the depths of vulnerability, and the more men learn how to embrace that, the more men will begin to become real men instead of caricatures of men.

It's time to break free from the cultural pressures that discourage men from talking honestly. Remember when we talked about the dangers of suppression? Well, unexpressed feelings will also come out in unhealthy ways. When men don't talk, or feel unable to express feelings of tenderness, hurt, or grief, these will come out in other ways—as anger, irritability, or, in the most extreme cases, violence.

DEALING WITH GUILT AND SHAME

We love the myth of either-or designations. . . . Men are either
brave soldiers charging into battle or delicate flowers incapable
of contributing and therefore unworthy of the title "man." The
reality is that human emotions are dynamic and fluid . . . That
emotion you're tamping down is going to come out somewhere, and odds are that somewhere isn't going to be good.

—JEN O'RYAN, "YES, MEN REALLY DO NEED SAFE SPACES"

Guilt and shame go hand in hand. When I feel guilty because
I did something I shouldn't have, I tend to feel ashamed that I
didn't have the strength not to do it in the first place. Ever been
there? Men, have you ever said to yourself, "What is wrong
with me? I thought I was better than this." The guilt and
shame the Dog makes us feel can be crippling. This is one of
the reasons I decided to write this book: to help men deal with
the devastating effects of guilt and shame.

I feel ashamed to even admit this, but without transparency
there can be no transformation, so I'll tell you my truth. After
I married Meagan, I caught myself looking at another woman.
It was very casual, and I almost did it without thinking. Then I
caught myself and thought, *What are you doing?* I had no desire
for this woman. I was not interested in her in the least, but I
found myself checking her out almost instinctively. I immediately felt guilt, asking myself (almost berating myself), "How
could you do that?"

I love my wife. I have no desire to cheat or be with anyone else. So why in the world did I look at this other woman? After the guilt, the shame set in. I said to myself, "You're terrible, what's wrong with you?" In that moment, I literally hated myself. I love my wife, and I love the Lord, yet that wasn't enough to stop this behavior. At first I didn't know what to do about it.

Brené Brown, the *New York Times* bestselling author of *Daring Greatly: How the Courage to Be Vulnerable Transforms the Way We Live, Love, Parent, and Lead*, has spoken and written a great deal on the topic of men, vulnerability, and shame. She says that while women have their own burden of shame associated with conflicting messages, the message men encounter from every segment of our society is that weakness of any kind is shameful. Since vulnerability equals weakness in the eyes of many men, the preferred alternative is to block out all feelings of inadequacy and uncertainty.

Since I didn't know how to handle my shame, I buried it. I did anything I could not to feel it. I denied it. I distracted myself. Men hide shame so that it doesn't have to be felt. Shame is withering self-judgment, and it's painful. What happens when an untrained dog goes to the bathroom in the corner of the living room and not outside? It hangs its head and hides. It knows it's done wrong and that when the master comes home it's going to be punished. Men hide from shame over negative behavior. Men cover it up with bluster, denial, or more vice so it doesn't have to be felt.

But hiding is dangerous; isolation is one of the most effective tools to keep men in these negative emotions of guilt and shame. In basketball, you run an isolation play because you want to go one-on-one and break your defender down so you can score. When men are isolated from themselves or from others who can help, they become susceptible to breaking down emotionally, physically, and spiritually.

Men must shed their reluctance to talk about guilt and shame. Brown defines shame as the idea that "[t]here's something fundamentally wrong with me, that I'm unworthy of love." Guilt is remorse over something you've done. Your inner voice says, "You did a bad thing." Shame goes deeper. This is the difference between guilt and shame: while guilt is about what you did, shame is a personal judgment about who you are. Your inner voice says, "You're no good. You're worthless and a failure." Shame, left hidden and unexpressed, can turn to self-hatred or deep feelings of unworthiness. Not feeling worthy then leads to self-punishment with even more bad choices because—and I know how messed up this sounds, but it's true—in those moments of deep shame, we feel we only deserve the worst life has to offer.

Most men feel less-than in some way. Most men carry around broken pieces from their childhood. Some men have never quite gotten past the shame of being a nerd who got picked on in school, or being the guy who got ridiculed for not knowing how to talk to girls. I carry around the wounds of always feeling awkward and never quite fitting in. The twisted thing is that when men carry a burden of shame, they also *feel ashamed for being weak enough to feel that shame*!

It's a vicious cycle that needs to end if we're ever going to be whole, become Masters, and be the husbands, fathers, and men we're designed to be. We need safe spaces so we can express our shame, guilt, pain, and vulnerability.

THE BOX

Unexpressed emotions will never die. They are buried alive
and will come forth later in uglier ways.

—SIGMUND FREUD

The fight is raging in many men. That fight is happening in part because there's an inherent conflict between who men really are and who men have been conditioned to be. This war consciously and subconsciously impacts every man in ways that aren't always apparent. Not every man allows the Dog to get out of control, but I do believe every man is impacted by social conditioning. That conditioning is a result of the box society tries to force men into. I first learned about this box during my work with the Oakland Men's Project. Tony Porter, the CEO of A CALL TO MEN, has also done extensive teaching about the "Man Box." Here's an idea of what this box looks like:

The Box

If men don't meet the societal definitions of manhood, they aren't considered "real men." These are some of the words, ideas, and standards that create the box that break men, because no man is, or can be, entirely defined by these words, ideas, and standards.

MEN ARE

Strong	Powerful
Aggressive	Superior to women
Successful	Money-makers
In control	Violent
Certain	Tough
Over-confident	Angry
Stoic	Take charge

Starting in early childhood, men often get locked into a restrictive "box" of options that tells us how we are allowed to think, feel, and *be* as men. As boys grow into men, if they fail to conform to that narrow standard of what society thinks it means to be a man, they are often met with verbal, emotional, and physical abuse—often from fathers, stepfathers, uncles, and other adult men in their lives.

The Box paints a hard, bleak picture of manhood. Men are only "allowed" to be breadwinners, violent, mean, bullies, tough, angry, active, strong, successful, and in control of women. Men are "expected" to have no emotions, stand up for themselves, yell at people, not make mistakes, not cry, take charge, push people around, have lots of sex, not back down, and take care of others. Jay-Z told David Letterman that, "For a lot of us, especially where I grew up and men in general, we don't have emotional cues from when we were young. Our emotional cue is 'Be a man. Don't cry.'" He was discussing his song "Song Cry," in which he raps: "I can't see 'em comin' down my eyes, so I gotta make the song cry."

This model of manhood has no room for weakness, doubt, gentleness, vulnerability, compassion, self-deprecation, or, God forbid, femininity. It's the stereotype of the stoic male—every man as John Wayne or Clint Eastwood, or even played out in hip-hop with personas like Rick Ross or Future. These men are in charge and project a machismo that detests weakness.

Through the OMP, I learned that if men stay locked in the Box into adulthood, we may find ourselves tortured by destructive emotions like confusion, rage, fear, shame, loneliness, stupidity powerlessness, vulnerability, revenge, hopelessness, and worthlessness. Overwhelmed by these feelings, with no acceptable way to express our fears and doubts without feeling diminished, many men learn to express emotion in the only acceptable way: through violence.

Actor, comedian, and author Michael Ian Black wrote about the outdated model of masculinity in an impassioned op-ed for the *New York Times*: "America's boys are broken. And it's killing us." Black was writing in the aftermath of the shooting at Marjory Stoneman Douglas High School in Lakeland, Florida:

> [M]anhood is measured in strength, where there is no way to be vulnerable without being emasculated, where manliness is about having power over others. They are trapped, and they don't even have the language to talk about how they feel about being trapped, because the language that exists to discuss the full range of human emotion is still viewed as sensitive and feminine.

Men, there is nothing feminine or sensitive about expressing emotion. That is a lie and a myth that keeps us trapped, unable to feel secure enough to express how we really feel. If Jesus wept, doesn't that give us permission to do the same? The very essence of manhood is found in the true expression of feelings—not in the absence of them.

Battling Brokenness

We came to see that boys and girls are hurt as children, vio-
lated, and rendered powerless. They are recipients of adult,
primarily male, violence. Boys are taught to pass on the
violence to others. Girls are expected to become victims of this
violence.

—PAUL KIVEL, *MEN'S WORK: HOW TO STOP*
THE VIOLENCE THAT TEARS OUR LIVES APART

In the Box, society tells young males that being a man means
being a conqueror, being tough, and not showing emotion.
Many men in adolescence were (and still are) abused verbally,
physically, or sexually if they didn't conform to these narrow
norms. Mocked as wimps (or worse), many were bullied or
beaten by male authority figures that wanted to "make men out
of us."

The Box breaks young men with childhood trauma, and
that trauma has consequences later in life. The CDC-Kaiser
Adverse Childhood Experiences (ACE) Study, a seminal public
health study, showed that childhood trauma—physical, sexual,
or emotional abuse, or witnessing the abuse of others, in addition to neglect or losing a parent—dramatically increases the
risk of chronic disease, mental illness, being a victim of violence, or acting violently later in life.

When boys are raised in traumatic environments, not only
does that increase the chances that they will become abusive or
violent toward women as adults, but it also increases the odds

that they may also abuse their own children, which could turn them into either future victims or abusers. We become broken, sometimes so badly that repair will take a lifetime.

What we call "toxic masculinity" today is men acting out their own brokenness. Most men are broken in some way, and most struggle to find ways to heal or keep these broken parts from being revealed. However, some men have histories of abuse, neglect, or other trauma so severe that they carry around crippling burdens of rage, self-loathing, and shame. Their experiences produce a feeling of complete, irreparable brokenness.

With no appropriate way to express these emotions (none that's acceptable in the context of what it means to be a man in our society, anyway), these feelings get suppressed. But feelings are like seeds. Bury them as deeply as you want, they'll still claw their way to the surface.

When they do, we often try to escape the pain by losing ourselves in something pleasurable. One of the most basic human needs is the need to feel good about ourselves. If men can't get that feeling from within, it will be sought from outside in the easiest, fastest way possible, which is often the most destructive way too.

Acquiring wealth, chasing after power, and engaging in meaningless sex are all ways men try to heal the brokenness and feel good, just for a little while. Because our culture insists that men shouldn't confront emotional fears, deal with abandonment issues, or open up about trauma, men can often feel that their only choice is to shut down emotionally and subscribe to whatever the culture mandates. But owning those emotions is exactly what men have to do to heal and train the Dog for good.

Most men carry something broken inside. But when men get together we're usually more interested in throwing shade at each other, having a good time, and talking up how we're crushing life and work than finding out how we're really doing. But in truth, as men, we need to open up more than we think. It all starts with this one simple question: How are you really doing?

Women, I can't say this enough: not one word in this chapter is designed to excuse men's behavior. But the Dog gets loose for a reason, and understanding why can make a real difference. You can help the man in your life confront his own brokenness by not letting him off the hook about his issues. Does he have a problem with his father? Was he abused as a child? Talk kindly but firmly with him about what's going on in his spirit, and don't let him dodge the conversation. If there's unresolved pain or conflict that he's not dealing with, opening up about it with you or a therapist could be the key. If he won't talk to you, find someone trustworthy that he will talk to, and encourage him to go.

Men, do you know what's broken in you and why?
What process do you need to undergo to fix it?

Boys Won't Be Boys

Another idea that perpetuates brokenness is "boys will be boys." After so much time, many men and some women have come to believe the lie that bad behavior is part of what *makes them men*.

"Boys will be boys." "That's just locker room talk." "Sow your wild oats." These sayings have contributed to infidelity, broken families, harassment, assault, and divorce.

It is time we redefine what it means to be a man. The "boys will be boys" excuse for bad behavior must end. As I've said, men have been living the high life on the "boys will be boys" credit card. Now, the bill is coming due, and the balance is *high*.

"Boys will be boys" perpetuates a vicious cycle of men never having to bear the responsibility of their actions. Any behavior deemed unacceptable just gets written off with the idea that this is just the way men are. If we keep buying into this excuse, then accountability just becomes a suggestion, not a requirement, for true manhood. This is why for change to happen, accountability is a must.

In going off on the idea of "natural born cheaters," female blogger Ta-ning Connai of *Curly Nikki* echoes the feelings that many women have about men and our "boys will be boys" excuse: "Is the implication true that, 'Men will be men, boys will be boys?' . . . So you're telling me that men were . . . actually created to DESTROY their family with their insatiable sex drive and inability to have control over their animalistic instincts to do whatever they want, so their wives can lose all sense of themselves after all they've sacrificed isn't enough?!!!"

In an article for *Observer*, Selena Strandberg writes: "'Boys will be boys' is a logic that excuses or trivializes male behavior at all stages of their development. . . . It is a phrase that, in many ways, captures the root of gender inequality." It does this by reinforcing gender roles that are detrimental to men and women.

Boys are raised believing their actions (no matter how bad) are acceptable and just a normal part of their biology. Girls are raised believing they have no recourse but to accept this type of behavior.

In a post for The Good Men Project, Joanna Schroeder states, "Boys deserve more than to be stereotyped or disregarded. Society sells boys short when we propagate the myth that they simply cannot control themselves. It's time to lay 'boys will be boys' to rest, once and for all. For the benefit of both boys *and* girls."

I agree, let's put it to rest and let's raise up a new standard of manhood. Real manhood is about responsibility and accountability. Men, we can choose to be more than our urges. Women, you don't have to feel hopeless in this regard. It's possible for men to get control of the Dog and refuse to give addictive lust a purchase on their spirit. But if men are going to step up and reverse a pattern that's become ingrained in us as "part of being a man," we must first embrace being enough.

Fatherlessness

We've talked about the reality that most men have some form of brokenness, and many have never acknowledged or healed from it. Well, the deeper reality is that this brokenness is often inflicted on men by their fathers.

We're in something of a fatherhood crisis in this country. Sixty-three percent of people who commit suicide come from fatherless homes. Men who grow up without fathers are more likely to act out, abuse alcohol and drugs, have low self-esteem, have a hard time dealing with stress, and suffer from depression or anxiety. Men raised by physically or emotionally abusive fathers are more likely to become abusers themselves and to harbor the self-hatred that makes them desperate for ways to feel good about themselves—most often, through sex.

When a father isn't around to teach a boy how to be a man, or the only lessons he teaches are fear, domination, and humiliation, we shouldn't be surprised when the boy grows into a man who has no idea how to live in a world where he's expected to show love, vulnerability, and fidelity. I've shared with you my experiences surrounding my father. He died when I was nine and I've had to pretty much face my entire life without a father to turn to. Even today, the pain of not having him around still affects me. It took years of nurturing by my mother and the women in my family, and years of my own prayer, discipline, and development, to avoid becoming a statistic. Fathers have a powerful, irreplaceable impact on how their sons show up in the world as men.

This is why it's important for all men to take stock of their relationship with their dad, whether good or bad, because our behavior is directly linked to the quality of our relationship with our father. There's no getting around the influence fathers have on sons. Whether a man's father was a great influence on him, a terrible one, or somewhere in between, it's important to face the reality of the relationship in order to find healing. So much of men's brokenness comes directly from a difficult relationship with their dad.

I had so much anger growing up related to my relationship with my father. He died before I could ever work it out with him directly, but I was still forced to acknowledge my pain as I came into manhood. I chose to forgive my father for all he wanted to be but couldn't, and I expressed my gratitude to him, even in death, that he helped bring me into this world.

For the fatherless men reading this, I'm living proof that even if you don't have a father in your life you can become a success personally and professionally. Not having a father around doesn't have to derail your life. It's not easy to work through the wounds created when dad isn't around, yet it's possible. Don't be in denial about the anger or abandonment you feel. Acknowledge the feelings and commit to the process of working through them every day. That's the key to unlocking your full potential as a man.

Toughness versus "Enoughness"

Atelophobia (from Greek *atelès*, "imperfect" or "incomplete" and *phóbos*, "fear" or "panic"): the fear of not being good enough

I'm the middle child of three boys, so it's always been a little hard for me to fit in. That continued into my years at the University of Southern California, and even into my professional life. I've never really fit into a category (a passionate Christian who works in Hollywood . . . or a prominent Hollywood producer who's also a Christian . . . say what?), so to compensate

I began to focus on overachieving as a way to find acceptance from others, and more important, from myself. Yet I've found that the more I have achieved, the less I feel accepted.

I constantly feel driven to do more. I'm a film and television producer, an author, a motivational speaker, and a preacher, but it's never quite enough. I'm always battling that inner voice that urges me to do more—and do it better—while knowing that nothing I do can make me feel adequate. Every day, I struggle to remind myself that it's who I am, not what I do, that matters most.

Most men fight this internal war of *doing* versus *being*— *toughness* versus "*enoughness*."

Manhood is taught in terms of men doing, not in terms of men being. This is causing untold damage to men. How? Because men usually try to find worth in what we do, not in whom we are. What we do is external; who we are is internal. We all have a need to feel validated, that's a natural internal need. However, I believe that when we seek something external to fill the void that is internal, it will never work. Internal problems can't be fixed by focusing on external solutions. Men, think about it—we keep doing, buying, building, but ultimately despairing because it's not enough. It will never be enough. It can't be. Healing our brokenness can only come from less doing and more being.

The world doesn't need men to do more,
it needs men to do better.

There's a psychological concept known as *hedonic adaptation*. It says that when human beings experience increased pleasure, such as making more money, buying something new, or entering a new romantic relationship, our happiness increases. In a short time, however, we become dissatisfied with the new status quo and start craving something more. Get a raise and in a little while we want a bigger one. Buy the iPhone X and before long we start haunting the Apple rumor sites wondering when the next phone is coming out.

I'm no different from you. I've felt that same dissatisfaction. Even though I'm successful, I've found myself looking around, feeling unsatisfied. But then I catch myself. I remind myself that that's not reality; it's just the Dog preying on my peace.

In reality, I have an amazing life and career. God has blessed me in more ways than I can count. But without self-awareness, it's easy to let dissatisfaction grow and fester, turning first into resentment and then into a deep sense of self-loathing because I feel I'm not doing enough.

Men, we must do better at accepting the fact that we're enough, all by ourselves, because we were created to be enough. Money, cars, houses, women, accolades, and achievements don't have the power to validate us. When we do our work and practice being enough, whatever happens externally will just be a manifestation of the work we're doing internally.

Meagan appeared in a movie called *Love by the 10th Date*, and at the end of the film her character wrote "I Am Enough" on her hand. That mantra resonates with women; it's common in self-improvement circles because it carries a powerful message: *You are equal to the task of life just as you are. You already are who you need to be. God made you whole.*

Men, let's adopt this mantra. Let's start owning who we are. Being who we are, and who we were created to be, creates our worth. My brothers, you are enough right now, today, even in your brokenness.

It's time that true manhood be judged by "enoughness." The key to happiness and peace is who we are, not what we do. Yes, men can find great joy in what they do, and what they do can bring them happiness; however, if what they do isn't tethered to an internal feeling of "enoughness," any positive feeling they experience will only be temporary.

This won't be easy. Men, we have to break out of the Box and overcome society's brainwashing about what it means to be a man. That will mean defying peer pressure, potentially losing some friends, facing the terrors of our past, and learning to place a higher value on our character, spirituality, and intellect rather than on our work, income, and sex drive. But we can do this. Peace is possible.

The Dog only cares about doing,
the Master focuses on being.

When we shift the focus onto being the best version of ourselves, everything else will fall into place. However, when this isn't the focus, no amount of doing can suffice.

For the men reading this, if you struggle with violent emotions, anger, depression, compulsive behavior, or other, more serious problems, just talking to friends or family might not be enough. Seek professional counseling immediately, before it's too late. Being strong is admitting that you are weak. Here are some resources that can help:

- Men Overcoming Violence (menovercomingviolence.org)
- Men's Resource Center of West Michigan (menscenter .org)
- XXX Church (xxxchurch.com)
- GoodTherapy.org
- The Domestic Abuse Project (domesticabuseproject.com)

For women who are raising sons, it's critical to understand the pressure your sons are under, trying to figure out what it means to be a man and fight the restrictions the Box puts on them. Helping your sons realize they are enough is the first step in helping them become tough in the right ways.

CREATE A SAFE SPACE

A safe space is a support group that consists of two or more people who agree to support, listen to, and help one another through life's greatest challenges.

You can't create a safe space alone, because you need to find someone to talk openly and honestly with. A safe space can be a regular gathering where everyone is free to speak openly and everyone listens without judging, but it doesn't have be a physical location. A safe space can be created on a phone call, on Skype, through a text message or an email. The idea is to have at least one person a man deems safe to communicate with about the challenges of dealing with lust and any other pressures. The spirit of the safe space decrees that any man can reach out to someone else at any time when he's feeling weak, fearful, or guilty and find someone to listen and offer counsel. Also because it's sometimes hard for men to open up, I recommend someone in the group become the team leader/moderator to help initiate and facilitate conversation.

A safe space doesn't have to be a group of men, and a man can have more than one safe space. Some people are better at helping with certain problems than others so as many safe spaces as needed can be created.

A safe space can be found with the following types of people:

- a spouse
- a girlfriend
- a trusted family member
- a male best friend
- a therapist
- a men's group
- a recovery group
- a men's ministry group

A safe space must have ground rules, which I call "Safe Space Agreements":

- Use "I" statements (don't speak in the third person, own your thoughts).

- What is shared cannot be used against the person sharing.

- What's said in the space stays in the space.

- Listen. Don't judge.

- Be transparent. Transparency leads to transformation.

- Practice empathy, not sympathy.

- Be open (emotionally and spiritually).

A safe space is about creating a headspace where men need not fit into any model of masculinity and need not feel embarrassed or less masculine for expressing true feelings. In that state of mind, you can feel safe dropping the facade and talking about the most private, painful parts of yourself—the expectations men feel pressured to meet, the guilt over past sins that hurt the women in your life, things that happened in childhood, and the feelings and desires you may have never shared with another living soul.

When a man begins to implement this, an immense burden will fall from his shoulders because he can finally share his feelings about his father, his parents' divorce, his sexual problems, his fears about not measuring up to other men, his shame over indiscretions, or anything else that is haunting him. Through my work as an author and preacher, I have seen men open up to me in ways that made them weep like children. But they found joy in the release of all that pent-up fear and regret. The grief fades, but the joy and relief don't.

Having a safe space is what helped me get over the shame and guilt I had because of the Dog, and it helps me keep the Dog in check today.

Talk It Out

Men who aspire to be Masters will discover that a safe space works wonders, and all it takes is just one other person who agrees, who's open enough to say "I hear you."

Those three words get to the heart of why a safe space is so vital for men. A safe space lets a man be heard. I'm a Golden State Warriors fan (sorry Cavs and Rockets fans), and their mantra is "Strength in Numbers." I agree with this wholeheartedly. Men need to know that they are not alone. A safe space will help a man find strength in numbers. Other men are dealing with the same things.

Having a safe space is a powerful signal that men are committing to doing their work. Remember, becoming a Master is a process, not an instant transformation. Also remember, being open about shame doesn't change what happened or make it all right, but it does allow a man to forgive himself and accept God's forgiveness too.

A safe space can be a safety valve for sexual desires and fantasies a man doesn't want to act on but can't get out of his mind.

If he's obsessing over a certain woman, for example, it can be talked out in the safe space. Remember, acknowledging an urge takes away most of its power. A safe space can also be an extension of a man's conscience, reminding him of the consequences of acting on negative urges.

WOMEN ARE THE IDEAL SAFE SPACE

Basically, all women are nurturers and healers, and all men are
mental patients to varying degrees.
—NELSON DEMILLE, *THE GENERAL'S DAUGHTER*

The safest safe space for a man should be with the woman in his life (his wife or a girlfriend with whom he's in a committed relationship). If a man is fortunate enough to be in a relationship with a woman who encourages him to share his thoughts, be vulnerable, and talk about his failures and fears without feeling embarrassed or emasculated, that's ideal. This is the safest of all possible spaces.

Strong, lasting marriages are safe spaces for men and women. When both partners are equals, feel confident enough to be honest, and are committed to the long-term health of their marriage, nothing is off limits. When men can talk about the Dog, their urges, struggles, and fears, and be taken seriously without being judged, the peace they feel is great. Men, don't be afraid to talk to your woman about creating a safe space at home if you don't already have one.

This is critical for women: *it's important that you help create a safe space for your relationship.* Look at the ground rules for a safe space—one of the most important ones is no judgment. In order to take your relationship to the next level, practice intense transparency. Some women want men to be honest—until she hears what he's being honest about. He says something she doesn't want to hear about lust or checking out other women, and she judges him for it.

A safe space means you might hear some things you don't want to hear, or learn things you didn't want to know about your man. But if your man needs to express it, love him enough to listen and take it in without getting upset and jumping down his throat. Brené Brown, interviewed in *The Atlantic* by Andy Hinds, says that, ironically, the shame men feel when we do reveal weakness or vulnerability is often inflicted by women: "Most women pledge allegiance to this idea that women can explore their emotions, break down, fall apart—and it's healthy . . . But guys are not allowed to fall apart."

I'm familiar with situations where a man opened up to a woman and she was so appalled at what he said that he never felt safe opening up to her again. When a man is trying to be better, that deserves respect. Shame a man who's trying hard and opening up to you—which is an act of courage—and you might lose him forever. If you can't handle intense transparency in your relationship, that places a limit on how far your relationship will go. If you can handle true, honest transparency, the man in your life will feel loved and accepted—and I guarantee that this will create a deep strength and mutual respect in your relationship that will help you go the distance.

However, if a man's girlfriend or spouse is unwilling to create a safe space where he can be vulnerable and express himself, the Dog will find a new safe space. This can happen inadvertently. I don't believe that most men intentionally seek out a place to feel safe, yet I do believe that deep down men are always looking for protection and validation. So if his needs aren't being met or he senses chaos in the home, a man might consciously or subconsciously seek out acceptance and validation wherever they can be found. That space may be with another woman who provides the intimacy the man isn't getting in his relationship. Doesn't make it right or justifiable, but I'm telling you the truth.

As we've discussed, when basic emotional needs are not met in our relationship, we become vulnerable to another person who seems ready to help meet those needs. In *His Needs, Her Needs*, Dr. Willard Harley writes, "Husbands' and wives' needs are so strong that when they're not met in marriage, people are tempted to go outside marriage to satisfy them." The irony is that the new space a man creates with another woman isn't safe at all. It's an *unsafe* space.

Here's what I mean. If a man feels like the woman in his life doesn't listen to his concerns or respect his feelings he may not be thinking about cheating on her, but he's unhappy. Then, he strikes up an innocent friendship with a female coworker. He enjoys talking with her; she listens to him in a way his wife doesn't, and he finds himself sharing more and more intimate details about himself and his feelings.

By this point in the book, you know this is the red zone for any man. It's dangerous for him to allow any woman who's not his wife or girlfriend to meet his emotional needs, even if it seems innocent, because the Dog will start to crave that intimacy. If he continues to confide in this woman, he will start to crave time with her and an emotional bond will form. One night he will be working late and emotional intimacy could become physical intimacy and the Dog will have begun to destroy his relationship.

Keep in mind that the infidelity in this scenario didn't happen when the man and woman had sex, but when the man chose emotional intimacy with someone other than his partner. When that happens, sex can almost seem inevitable. By that time, major damage is being done to all parties involved.

Men, emotional intimacy with any woman who's not your monogamous partner is an unsafe space.

This is why I don't believe a man should confide intimate details about his feelings to any woman who is not his wife, girlfriend, or family member. Female friends can still be friends, but a man must be cautious about how open he is with them (even female friends who were his best friend before he got married). It's easy to "catch feelings for each other" when you're sharing your deepest, darkest secrets.

Even when you're single, be careful how open you are with a female best friend. I've seen it happen. You're thinking, "Oh, we're just friends, we can talk about everything," but then once one of you starts dating someone, jealousy blindsides you. This can create a world of trouble, because appropriate boundaries for the friendship haven't been established. This is one of the reasons men need a "safe space mentality."

THE SAFE SPACE MENTALITY

A safe space mentality helps preserve the quality of safe spaces by making it clear when an unsafe space might be in the making. With a safe space mentality, a man trains himself to become hyperaware of the intimacy he's sharing with women who aren't his partner. This prevents a man from unintentionally falling into a situation that ultimately feeds the Dog, not the Master. Women, I also share this with you so you can be aware of when you are in a safe space—or potentially an unsafe space—with a man.

A safe space mentality works in concert with many of the ideas we discussed in the "Claim Your Territory" chapter. When men employ a safe space mentality, it helps heighten their awareness when they're talking to a woman at work, the gym, via text or online, and confiding in her in a way that creates a dangerous level of intimacy. Using this mentality helps a man learn to identify anyone outside his monogamous relationship who is meeting his emotional needs and take steps to alter the dynamics of that relationship—or possibly, just be safe and end it.

I've said that any woman who is not a man's wife, girlfriend, or family member should not be meeting his emotional needs. But let's go a step further. For a safe space mentality to work, a man must admit to himself that any female friend he finds attractive and that is also a great listener is probably someone he should limit spending lots of alone time with. He should also monitor the tenor of the conversation. We shouldn't put ourselves in a situation that could lead us to fail.

Men, be on the lookout for interactions with women that make you feel heard, understood, validated, and even desired. If any of these women are not your wife or girlfriend, proceed with caution. Ask yourself, "Why aren't I experiencing these same desirable feelings with my wife/girlfriend? What's wrong with that relationship, and can it be repaired?" These are important questions to ask yourself because maybe there's something you need that you're not getting in your relationship that could be fixed. This way, you'll get what you need emotionally from the relationship you're in. The safe space mentality is a lens through which you can view all your female relationships and put them in perspective so that you can maintain your growth toward Mastery.

BE A SAFE SPACE

So a man is not a man when he is created; he is only begun.
His manhood must come with years. He that goes through life
prosperous, and comes to his grave without a wrinkle, is not
half a man. Difficulties are God's errands and trainers, and
only through them can one come to the fullness of manhood.
—HENRY WARD BEECHER

If we as men need a safe space, then we must also *be* a safe space for every man and woman we come in contact with. It's long past time to write a new definition of what it means to be a man that includes creating safety for both men and women. One of the most important shifts that *must* happen in the wake of the sexual assault stories that have been appearing all over the country is in men's belief that violence against each other or against women in any form is ever acceptable. The culture of manhood says violence is one of the ways that men act manly, but, as I've noted, that puts all men, boys, women, and girls at risk.

It's time to delete that attitude. Workplace harassment and domestic violence are terrible threats to women, and they have no place in Mastery. There is no excuse for a man raising his hand to a woman, touching her in a way that makes her feel threatened, or threatening violence against her. *Ever*.

Real men don't threaten or commit acts of violence against women. Real men don't call women shameful names. Jay-Z even admitted to the *Wall Street Journal* that some of his lyrics were out of line, saying, "Some [lyrics] become really profound when you see them in writing. Not 'Big Pimpin'.' That's the exception. It was like, I can't believe I said that. And kept saying it. What kind of animal would say this sort of thing? Reading it is really harsh."

Real men are masters of their tempers; their tempers do not master them. Men who commit any kind of violence against women, or who intimidate or exploit women in any way, are not men but cowards. If you have a problem with anger or violence, don't just seek a safe space. Seek professional counseling now.

Being a safe space for others means that we men must manage our desires so we can control them, not selfishly service them in a way that makes everyone around us collateral damage in our pursuit of pleasure. Men, we have to be a safe space, especially for women. It's not enough for them to just be a safe space for us. How comfortable do we allow them to feel around us? We have to create an environment where any woman who gets close to us won't feel uncomfortable. Part of doing our work is not allowing our frustrations, anger, resentments, or anxieties to be taken out on anyone. The safety of others in our presence must become a primary concern. If there's anything you are doing that makes those around you feel unsafe emotionally, physically, or spiritually, STOP. Reassess. Pray. Get help. Be a safe space.

CHAPTER 8

REPAIR THE DAMAGE

Love never dies a natural death. It dies because we don't know
how to replenish its source. It dies of blindness and errors and
betrayals. It dies of illness and wounds; it dies of weariness, of
witherings, of tarnishings.

—Anaïs Nin, French essayist

As we discussed in chapter 1, an untrained dog is a dangerous
dog. Dogs that haven't been trained put themselves and everyone they come in contact with at risk. Even when a dog has
been trained there can be lapses in their behavior; they may destroy property, or, in some cases, bite. The cost of the damage a
dog can create is much more than you might think. According
to the Insurance Information Institute and State Farm insurance, "Dog bites and other dog-related injuries accounted for
more than one-third of all homeowners liability claim dollars
paid out in 2017, costing almost $700 million." In 2017 there
were 18,522 claims, with an average cost of roughly $37,000 per
claim.

In the case of dogs and their owners, insurance handles the
vast majority of damage a dog causes. But what do we do when

the Dog leads a man to wreak havoc? How do we repair that damage?

All the discipline, self-awareness, and prevention men undertake can't undo what's been done, but there are things that can be done to try and make it better. A March 2018 *Deadline: Hollywood* article explored just how costly the damage has been: it stated that the Time's Up Legal Defense Fund, which had launched two months earlier and aims at helping individuals who experience sexual misconduct, including assault, abuse, or harassment find legal representation, had not only raised $21 million in just that time alone, but fielded inquiries from 1,700 women across sixty industries ranging from Silicon Valley tech companies to the military.

This is just one example of how the damage the Dog does is being addressed. I'm going to primarily focus on infidelity in this chapter because that's where the Dog hits closest to home, but keep in mind that this is not the only place the Dog causes problems. When the Dog gets loose, it creates real damage, but the experts I talked with said that as often as fifty percent of the time, a marriage can be saved with the right assistance if both the man and woman want to make it work. The chewed-up sofa can be fixed, the shredded shoes mended, the holes in the yard filled—but men have to be the ones to accept responsibility for what they have done wrong and do whatever it takes to begin repairing the damage.

In the following sections I highlight two fascinating interviews my writing partner and I conducted with men brave enough to share their stories about how they have reformed their Dog ways.

CONFESSIONS OF A
SELF-PROCLAIMED "MAN-WHORE"

Anton Ross, fifty-two, an Internet marketer in Alameda, California, was nice enough to talk to me about his life as what he cheerfully calls a "man-whore." A military brat who lived all over the world as a kid, the combination of no sexual discipline and a ravenous sexual appetite led him to two ill-advised marriages, two divorces, numerous affairs, and enough drama and chaos for ten men. Now, in a stable relationship with his wife, Laura, he says he finally understands why the Dog ran wild for so many years—and finally craves the peace that eluded him for so long.

"I'm pretty certain the two main driving forces in my behavior were an early sexual awakening, and a lifetime spent leaving every place I've called home," he says. "At an early age, I started experimenting with my sexuality. It wasn't stigmatized in the permissive countries I grew up in like it was in the U.S. By the fifth grade I'd already had my first sexual experience, with a girl of the same age. We lived on the NATO base in Keflavík, Iceland, and had a lot of freedom, especially during those long summer nights.

"And then in seventh grade, we left," Anton continues. "Naples, Italy, was the next exotic location we were to call home, and so we boarded an ancient U.S. Navy cargo plane and left the Arctic Circle for warmer climes. While living in Italy, we spent many Sunday dinners with our extended family, and being the *cugino americano* [American cousin] made me a person of interest to a number of my female cousins. Needless to say, there was a lot of flirting and other semi-childish games. There were a few American and English girls who cycled in and out of my life, but they were really setting the stage for more adventures as I got older.

"Then in tenth grade, we left," he goes on. "Sensing a pattern? More moves to various parts of the States followed, each lasting no more than a few years. I think each time I was grasping for a sense of belonging that a life constantly in motion denied me.

"Throughout my teens, twenties, thirties, and forties, I basically carpe diemed my way through life," Anton says. "More than a few of my former girlfriends are still friends, and the majority of the breakups I experienced (or caused) were amicable. I wasn't reckless with the women who circled in my orbit—at least I tried not to be. But I'm not sure I was trying to satisfy anything more than my own carnal desire to live life to the fullest.

"But now, things are different," he concludes. "Laura is a special breed. She's highly educated, with an artist mother and a father who teaches at Brown. She's attractive, well traveled, exceptionally intelligent, and strangely, a total introvert. I'm not sure I consciously decided to do things differently with her; I believe I've just finally matured to the point where my priorities have changed. We've just passed the six-year mark together, and things 'just work' with us. My family and friends adore her, and the two of us make time to relate to each other and do the little things that add up and make a relationship work. She also has a sense of adventure, which we're about to put to the test as we prepare for a live-aboard life on a Catalina 42 sailboat in the Bay Area. After all these years, and all those women, I can't imagine being with anyone else."

INSIGHTS FROM A REFORMED PLAYER

A real man isn't an unchained libido—a rabid Dog. A real man squares his shoulders, bravely confronts who his choices have made him, and owns up to the wounds he's inflicted and the cost he's borne. Then he takes action to start making different choices, knowing that different choices equal different outcomes.

That's exactly what Albert Rocker, twenty-nine, did after a few years of living the wild life in Los Angeles. Rocker, a devout Christian and the author of *Do It Anyway*, moved to LA in 2011 after graduating from Georgia Tech, where he played football and earned a business degree that landed him a job at Microsoft. Living in downtown LA at twenty-two, a single, fit ex-athlete with more money than he knew how to spend, he did what a lot of young guys in that position would have done: He went clubbing with his friends and got with women. Lots of women.

"When I moved to LA, I had an idea of the lifestyle I was supposed to be living," he says. "An idea that was conditioned from childhood. Guys always heard, 'You go from the ball field to the bedroom to the boardroom.' Men had to be successful in each one of those areas to be considered masculine. That's where a lot of our expectations for ourselves come from. We've been conditioned, and we don't have an opportunity to challenge those thoughts.

"I had been successful playing college football at Georgia Tech, but I no longer had that fulfillment," Rocker continues. "So I moved on to the next phase, which is to be the best in the bedroom. I started chasing after that without even knowing why. The idea was to sleep with as many women as I could. No man would ever ask me, 'Why are you doing that?' because they thought it was normal. We would go to the club two or three times a week and invest a lot of money in table service, which earned us the credibility to pretty much walk into whatever club we wanted on any night. And pretty much any woman I wanted to, I could take home and have sex with. I almost never saw the same woman twice. I mean, you didn't have to.

"That carried on for months," Rocker goes on. "This was Los Angeles, so at clubs we'd meet celebrities or people with fancy homes, and we'd end up going from a club to a house party, where things would get really crazy. I had three years caught up in a lifestyle and I didn't even really know what I was doing. It was the lifestyle every man dreams of, except I was at a point in my career and my sexuality and just in life in general where I was so unfulfilled, and I finally started asking myself why."

Rocker says his growing sense of emptiness and lack of fulfillment coincided with a work-related move down to Orange County, south of LA. This gave him the opportunity to be alone, get off the club-women-sex roller coaster, and reflect on what he was doing and why he felt the way he did.

"That was the most crucial thing, because when you're alone with your thoughts, you start thinking about why you do some of the things you do," he says. "At the same time that I was able to start unpacking my thoughts and behaviors, I picked up a couple of books by Brené Brown, *The Gift of Imperfection* and *Daring Greatly*. From them, I started to learn about the concept of shame. I started understanding how shame prevents people from both loving themselves and loving others.

"It's tricky, because most of the time when someone says, 'Hey, you're just ashamed,' you're like 'No, that's not me,'" Rocker continues. "But when you really understand what shame is and how powerful it is and how it influences everybody's behavior, no matter who you are, you'll start to become aware of it in your life. That takes being super honest with yourself. When I was able to do that, I saw that I didn't have a purpose at that time. I thought I was living for the women, the cars, the money, and the materialistic things, but when I acquired all that stuff it was as if I had achieved nothing.

"I finally saw that a lot of it came from my childhood," he goes on. "If you think about the core of most men's promiscuous behavior, I think it revolves around childhood issues of confidence and love. If a man's happily married and he feels like he has to step out on his wife, he feels the need for approval. He's trying to feel like he's still 'got it' or feel validated in some way. When I thought about it from that perspective, I think a lot of the shame I was experiencing came from my early struggles to get along with my father.

"My father was a drill sergeant in the army, and that generation of men, they were taught to love a different way," Rocker says. "They were taught to love in their own language, which was 'Hey, I provide for my family. I make sure my child has what he needs.' But if the people that you expect to love you a certain way don't show you that love, it affects you. Any man who tells you it's not affecting him is lying. He hasn't dealt with it. In my case, I thought I could skip from childhood to adulthood and not deal with some of the traumatic experiences I experienced in my relationship with my dad. But there are no shortcuts.

"I felt shame about those childhood experiences, and Brené Brown said that massive shame can lead to the disowning of self, leading to self-sabotage, addiction, or high sexual appetite," he notes. "Basically, you want to be loved so much that you'll give yourself to anybody. I can tell you as a man who has probably been at the peak of my sexual life, in terms of sleeping with the most gorgeous women I'm ever going to sleep with and the most women I'm ever going to sleep with, I still got no fulfillment from that."

Another pivotal event in Rocker's transformation came when he rode with a married friend to Las Vegas. "From the outside, you would think he was happily married," he says. "He had a brand-new child. Then he started telling me about his lifestyle and all the women he was sleeping with. I started to realize that if I kept on doing what I was doing, I would end up being who he is. I had always had this idea in my mind that whenever I met the right woman, I would just stop. At that moment, I realized that it's not like that, because he told me. He said, 'Yo, it doesn't stop when you're married. You just get to choose whether you want to engage with it or not.' I thought, 'That's a pretty troubling way to live.'

"I said, there has to be a different way," he continues. "I never wanted to be so out of control that my family was in jeopardy. I came to the realization that I had to make a change. Although I was sold on the idea of changing, I didn't really know how, so I just started developing different disciplines. I deleted every woman I was sleeping with from my phone and blocked them. It didn't matter if I'd had a conversation with them the day before. Everybody on the list went away at the same time. I needed to do something to shake up my world and change my habits. That started making me more conscious of my choices and my behaviors. Then I decided I wouldn't get any numbers from new women. It was pretty simple: if I can't text them or call them, I won't have sex with them. Then I started practicing those behaviors and then I started to change my perceptions and my mind-set. Slowly but surely my mind started to renew and I started seeing things a little bit differently."

That shock of self-awareness also got Rocker thinking about what *would* give him fulfillment, and that started him down a new course for his life. He's now been celibate for three years, written his book, and started a nonprofit, Aspire Beyond, to help inspire people to chase their dreams.

"Now that I understand, I see things from a different perspective," he says. "Now that I don't yearn for the love of the world, God's the only one who I seek love from. Everything else is gravy. Everything else is cool if it happens. But that's not where I'm deriving my value from. I forgave myself. It didn't even have to do with my father anymore because at that point I had already accepted that I had everything I needed."

MEN CHEAT AT A HIGHER RATE THAN WOMEN

The responsibility for repairing the Dog's damage begins with the man, as we created the problem to begin with. The burden of figuring out how to rebuild trust and communication can't be laid at the wife's or girlfriend's feet.

Any man owes it to the woman he's wronged to do whatever it takes to show her that he is fully accountable, deeply remorseful, and that he feels torn up inside for having caused her such pain. He has to show her that he will do anything to make it right and earn back her trust. Does that mean consenting to being in closer contact—checking in frequently via FaceTime on business trips, or leaving his phone out and unlocked? *It could.* Does that mean he's the one to make an appointment with a marriage counselor? *It might.* Does that mean accepting the accusing stares and angry words from her friends, her siblings, and her parents without a word? *It will.*

Men, if you've cheated, be prepared to do it all while remaining fully aware that your lady may well reject your efforts, move out, and slam the door on any reconciliation. That's the risk you took when you engaged in cheating. The road back, if there is one, is long and not easy. Everything depends on you being totally committed, surrendering your pride, and holding nothing back.

"Men cheat at a significantly higher rate of frequency than women," says Dr. Fran Walfish, Beverly Hills family and relationship psychotherapist, author of *The Self-Aware Parent*, and regular expert child psychotherapist on *The Doctors* (CBS TV). "Men become serial cheaters because of early abandonment or separation trauma by their mother or father. Examples include divorce, a parent leaving and not returning, or an angry parent who rages toward the child unexpectedly and abusively (physically or verbally). Women cheat when they have sustained long periods of mistreatment in the relationship.

"In both male and female cheating," she continues, "there's a lack of healthy communication skills to talk about the underlying problems and issues within the relationship that, if dealt with directly, could help prevent infidelity.

"If a man cheated only one time, and demonstrates genuine remorse, regret, empathy, and he apologizes to his wife, solemnly promising to never ever cheat again, a 'sex pass' can be allowed and the breach of trust can be repaired with two willing partners," Dr. Walfish concludes. "Based on my professional experience, a small percentage of men who have cheated more than once reform. I have, however, seen a positive turnaround occur when the cheater demonstrates genuine remorse for hurting his spouse and immersing himself in psychotherapy treatment in a completely committed fashion."

HOW DO YOU FIX A RELATIONSHIP AFTER CHEATING?

Many of the men I counsel and speak with all want to know the same thing: Is healing possible? We've all heard friends and family members proclaim that after they were cheated on, they could never trust the other person again. Once a cheater, always a cheater, right? But is that really true? Can there be repair, rehabilitation, and restoration of a marriage after infidelity? Can men who've been unrepentant players really change their ways and start treating women not as sex toys but as people?

The answer is, it depends. It depends on the circumstances and what kind of damage has been done. It depends on whether the infidelity was a one-time mistake or a pattern going back years. It depends on how committed the man and woman are to making things work and getting past the crisis, as Jason Weis, a family law attorney at Curran Moher Weis, says.

"Of our adultery cases, probably seventy-five percent are men," he writes in an email. "It's a big generalization, but the couples who tend to survive adultery are those who have longer relationships and limited adulterous behavior (e.g., an isolated indiscretion). Successful couples are able to prioritize the larger benefits of their relationship over the benefits of an unblemished record of fidelity. They look past a single sexual act and choose to preserve a relationship that has greater benefits for them emotionally, socially, professionally, financially, etc., and has similar benefits for their children.

"Long-term infidelity, waste of family assets with paramours, dangerous/stupid behaviors with the paramours, and repeated acts of deception or dishonesty are behaviors that tend to ensure that the relationship fails. In such circumstances, the sense of betrayal cuts so deep that it becomes fatal to rational behavior."

In other words, to save the relationship, both the man and woman have to want to save it. That's a hard sell when infidelity is a longtime pattern. In such cases, especially if the man has been caught cheating in the past, promised to reform, and then sinned again, the marriage is likely over.

Trust is like an antique vase: slow and difficult to build, distressingly easy to shatter, and nearly impossible to mend. If a man has already cheated and isn't willing to become accountable to his woman and completely change his ways—and more important, if he doesn't get control of the lust within—it's very likely he'll cheat again. After all, according to Trustify, "People who have cheated before are 350 percent more likely to cheat again." That brutal number reflects a brutal reality.

But a relationship can be repaired, and if a man is blessed enough to be married to or dating a woman who really wants things to work out, it's definitely easier. Author Stacey Greene wrote her book, *Stronger Than Broken: One Couple's Decision to Move Through an Affair*, to share what she learned in repairing her marriage after her husband's infidelity. Speaking with me, she was quite candid about her role in the problems that nearly tore their union apart more than six years ago when she caught him texting his mistress.

"I know it went on for about six months, but when people say, 'once a cheater, always a cheater,' that's a lie. I don't ever think he would do it again and I don't think he ever did it prior to that. I think he was very lonely. We were at a gap point in our marriage, more like roommates with benefits. He went and did his thing and I went and did mine, and there was too much autonomy in the relationship. He was out with his guy friends, and I was off working extra jobs and doing things with my girlfriends, and never the twain did meet.

"When he agreed to see our pastor, I assumed he would want to fix it because biblically, you don't divorce," she continues. "But the first thing the pastor said was, 'What do you think? Do you still love her? Do you want to fix it?' When my husband said yes, I knew there was hope. Because there was still love there, it was fixable. I was also raised in a great home with two goofy-in-love parents, and because my father raised me in the Christian faith I really felt like since Jesus forgave all those other people's sins, I can certainly forgive some sins.

"The way we did it was a little out of the ordinary, though," Greene goes on. "Most people see therapists and counselors, and we didn't want to go to one. We're just really stubborn, competitive people, and I think this was just about our own stubbornness and desire to fix it. We read a lot of relationship books, including Gary Chapman's *The 5 Love Languages* and a wonderful book by Laura Doyle called *First, Kill All the Mar-*

riage Counselors. She talks a lot of about self-care and making yourself number one before you start to care for someone else.

"So, we worked through it," she concludes. "But it was hard. It took almost a year before I stopped crying every night. But it was miraculous, because by us reading these books to each other and doing the silly exercises and taking the tests, we realized that even though we had been married for twenty-five years, we weren't always addressing each other's real needs. Now, we've learned how to date each other again after all those years. I look forward to date nights now."

Wall Up the Window and Practice Radical Honesty

For a terrific understanding of how to fix a relationship after cheating, Dr. Shauna Springer spoke about two very powerful concepts, the first having to do with the "wall" that exists around strong marriages. Remember what I said earlier about not allowing another person to satisfy your emotional needs outside the relationship? Dr. Springer uses a slightly different metaphor and suggests not opening a "window" to someone else (a concept she says was inspired by the work of the late Shirley Glass). When a window is opened, the security of the relationship is breached and an outsider is given a look inside. From there, it's much easier to let that person inside the walls of the relationship, so to speak, and that's when the affair begins.

Dr. Springer says, "What needs to happen to repair a relationship is that you have to wall up that window with the affair partner by setting firm, clear, transparent boundaries—making

sure that there's no more window, and making sure that's clear
to the one who's been hurt. You have to open up the window
to your marriage partner again in a much deeper way than before. Functionally, what that means is that you have to have the
courage to engage in radical honesty with your spouse." This is
similar to what I call intense transparency.

"What people want to know depends on the relationship,"
she continues. "The injured partner may not want to know
very much other than when the affair started, how long it went
on, and the steps that have been taken to wall up that window.
They also need to know if there's anything they need to shift in
the relationship to make sure that they restore the intimacy that
both people need.

"Other people need to know everything," she says. "They
need to know details, like what the infidelity involved and
where it occurred, because they need to know that nobody
outside the marriage knows something about their partner that
they don't know. It keeps their anxiety in check if they have
real information and they're not filling the gaps of what they
don't know with information that's not true, which then ramps
up their anxiety and distrust. The person who committed the
affair needs to have the courage to share whatever the injured
partner needs to know, at whatever level the injured partner
needs to understand it."

That's brilliant. Dr. Springer is also an advocate of an incredible tool: *radical honesty*. "Going forward, the couple have
to renew their bond in a way that includes radical honesty,
which is based on Peggy Vaughan's (deceased expert in the

area of extramarital affairs) work," she says. "That means I will tell you every time I feel an attraction—that cocaine rush—to somebody outside the marriage, I will tell you immediately, because it's secrecy that fuels affairs. It's combustible. But the minute they share the attraction with their spouse, it loses its power. You start to notice flaws in the person you were attracted to. If you don't engage in radical honesty, you continue to idealize the affair partner, and things grow in secrecy."

I know. This is a bold and daring practice. I'm sure most can't imagine going home and telling their spouse, "Baby, I have to tell you about who I saw at the gym today! Mmm-hmmm!" This might sound extreme, but extreme problems cause for extreme measures! Dr. Springer uses it in her own marriage.

"Here's how I use radical honesty in my marriage," she says. "I had a new coworker who I just thought was great. I was attracted to him initially, and the minute he came onboard, I went home to my husband and said, 'I have a new coworker; here's his name. I had a feeling of attraction to him, which I know is based on absolutely nothing other than the fact that I'm really grateful to have somebody on board who cares about the same things I do. I'm telling you this because I love you and I know that as soon as I say this he'll be another coworker to me. So I just wanted to let you know that I had that projection today, and I'm telling you because I care about you and our relationship more than anything else.'"

Wow. That's powerful. The key, Dr. Springer says, is to be open about attraction early, when it doesn't mean anything.

Then your partner won't be threatened; they'll see that as your way of having their back and defending the marriage.

This can work for both men and women. Can you see how potent radical honesty can be? What would happen if the next time you felt an attraction to someone at work, you went home and told your spouse about it in the context of letting them know because you want to turn the attraction into something mundane, something they don't have to worry about? Since the context of infidelity is all about secrets and lies, coming clean like that could change everything. Try it.

Get Help

But don't be fooled. When a man has let the Dog rip apart everything he cares about, it's an emergency situation. If he wants to save the relationship, that means two things. First, get help. Second, get help now.

Elisabeth Goldberg, a New York–based marriage and family therapist and dating coach, is emphatic that repairing a relationship after infidelity is not a do-it-yourself situation. "You can't do it on your own," she says. "It will resurface. It will manifest into other things, and it will destroy your marriage. It's like saying, 'I want to heal from cancer on my own. I don't want to use medicine. I don't want to go to a doctor.' That's how serious it is. It's an illness. It's an emergency. If you have a crisis and you're bleeding to death, what do you do? You go to the ER. You cannot fully heal without the help of a relationship therapist."

When it comes to the hard work, Goldberg is blunt. Men, she says, need to be ready to take some hits and humble themselves if they're going to have any hope of healing. They can praise their women more in front of their friends. They can make self-deprecating jokes around others, and especially around their partner. They have to be real with it. They have to own it. They have to not be afraid to talk about it. They have to not be afraid to ask their wives, "How are you feeling about this?"

Practice Adoration

Goldberg suggests that men should plan on overcompensating with adoration for their wives while at the same time taking the brunt of the pain on themselves. "He has to reassure the woman that she has a lot of integrity for giving him another chance, that she's a strong woman, and that she can have the space to express her anger," she says. "But he has to always intervene with a proclamation of his devotion to her and his appreciation for her compassion, and of his despair and self-disgust with his behavior. He needs to show a lot of validation for the pain she is going through and take it all upon himself before they can really start dealing with why this happened.

"He needs to show her every which way that he puts her needs first," she continues. "He needs to go to extremes. He needs to say, 'Do you want me to check in with you every hour?' while he's at work. He needs to reassure her of his availability, because women are going through a process of grief, and if men stay stuck in their shame and guilt, they don't externalize their love and support and appreciation for their woman's compassion. They make it about themselves and say, 'I don't want to think about it. I'll never do it again. Can we please move on?' That's poison to the woman's ears. She hears the man saying, 'I don't care about you and I'll do it again.'

"There has to be a period of exaggerated adoration, appreciation, and praise," Goldberg concludes. "The man needs to empower her because she's feeling like nothing—like her needs were completely neglected. His focus has to be on building her up."

Invite God into the Process

For a faith-based perspective on the hard work involved, we turn to Geremy Keeton, licensed marriage and family therapist. He writes in an email:

"Said in the simplest terms: Cut off the affair, fully own the wrong, and begin the relentless work—with counseling— to repair it. Don't take offense at a wife's initial anger if she's begun expressing it. It's not a time to be defensive or self-righteous. Bringing in outside help and having humility are essential for containment of the situation." Keeton goes on to say, "When recovery is done well there can actually be restoration of biblical proportion—and by that, I mean the kind of restoration that takes the marriage to an even stronger place than it ever was before the crash. Without a thorough 'no holds barred' approach to repentance and recovery, however, the damage can linger and be forever exploited by the enemy of our souls.

"That's why anyone who has cheated must unequivocally and fully cut off all ties with the other person(s)—this means cutting off physically, emotionally, and, oh yes, all social media contact too." I completely agree with Mr. Keeton, there has to be a complete disconnect from the other person. Not only will it help prevent another occurrence from happening, it will also help ease the nerves of the spouse that got cheated on. Disconnecting from the person is essential for the healing to begin.

He continues, "This gets to the next hurdle—the probability of 'withdrawal pains.' The affair is likely acting on the brain as an addiction. It's sin, and it's sin that is now intertwined in the brain and creating a biochemical 'high.' Stopping it leads to withdrawal and craving for the object or experience. Sexual sins often create what Hebrews 12:1 refers to when it mentions a 'sin which clings so closely' (ESV) or a 'sin which so easily and cleverly entangles us' (AMP). Once the mechanisms of addiction are in motion, stopping 'cold turkey' and by one's own sheer personal determination is unlikely—or even impossible. 'Sobriety' is unsustainable as a solo act.

"This means a man must enlist recovery support—and preferably from a compassionate professional who will help him discover the 'why' and the 'triggers' behind his affair. Typically, he has issues to excavate and begin to heal within his personal history (family of origin and sexual history). Also, the marriage relationship must be addressed. The marriage was somehow vulnerable to this occurring, and the dynamics between the couple need to be addressed. The non-offending spouse is never to be blamed for the cheating, but the wife is part of the recovery process if marital recovery is going to be had. A wife's wounds, as well as her way of functioning in the marriage prior to the affair, must both be understood if recovery is to be solid and healing complete." Prayer and committing to the process of repairing the damage can be a powerful combination for healing a broken relationship.

If you're a woman and you've been cheated on, I know there are no words to express the pain you feel. Once the damage is done, it becomes very difficult to put the pieces back together. No one can tell you exactly what to do, not even me. However, what I would suggest is to not make any rash decisions, take the time to collect yourself, pray, and assess the road ahead. Much of what I've tried to lay out in this chapter can give you the necessary tools to help you process how to best respond to the devastating betrayal of your love and trust. My prayers are with you as you navigate this situation and I want you to know you're not alone. You can rebuild, whether you choose to do so inside or independently of your current relationship.

FORGIVENESS

Forgiveness is one of the main aspects of repairing the damage. If you have committed an offense, I encourage you to seek forgiveness from the one you have offended. It's not enough to feel badly and not say anything. When you ask for forgiveness, you are accepting responsibility and accountability for your actions. An important thing to remember about seeking forgiveness is it's up to the person you've offended if they choose to give it or not. Don't become upset or frustrated if forgiveness isn't offered up speedily. Every person has to go through their process and depending on the level of the offense, the person you've offended has to decide if and when they want to offer forgiveness. You can only control what's in your control. Asking for forgiveness is within your control, receiving it is not.

When you've done something you aren't proud of, it's very easy to come to the conclusion "I'll never forgive myself." However, I would caution against this. Harboring unforgiveness can lead to perpetual guilt and shame that, as we've discussed, can be a recipe for even more negative behavior that you are trying to overcome. Forgiving yourself doesn't mean you absolve yourself of the remorse you feel when you acted out of character. No, when you forgive yourself, you acknowledge what you did and the remorse you feel can serve as a powerful catalyst to helping you make the commitment to work every single day to become a better person. We can choose to become better after we've done things we are ashamed of. I'm not a proponent of the old adage "forgive and forget." Forgiving yourself isn't a magic wand that washes all your sins away. Forgiving is important, yet remembering the bad things you've done can be healthy because those memories can serve as a deterrent to engaging in that behavior again.

HOW DO YOU FIX A CAREER AFTER IT'S DAMAGED?

I heard a saying once growing up: "Integrity is like virginity, once it's gone you can't get it back." There is some truth to this, especially in a career sense. If you pursue greed at all costs, you may end up doing things that damage your reputation, your integrity, your company, and potentially your family. Word of caution: there's some damage that can't ever be repaired. Think of Bernie Madoff; there's nothing that can ever be done to repair the damage to his image or career. Be that as it may, if you have found yourself in a situation that has hurt your career, here's what you can do to try to mitigate the damage.

1. Apologize always and often. When you've done something wrong, you may feel that once you've apologized for it then that should be it and you'll never have to do it again. Not so. Depending on the level of your offense, don't become offended when people bring it up continually or if you feel you must keep seeking forgiveness. The more consistently contrite you are, the better the chances you have of communicating the sincerity of your remorse to those you need to reestablish credibility with the most.

2. Get to the root. Don't be satisfied with making apologies just for what you did wrong. Go through the process of getting counseling and professional help to get to the root of what's going on in you that created the behavior to begin with.

3. Make personal recovery your primary goal, not just professional recovery. What I mean is that when you've done something that has taken a negative toll on your career, your knee-jerk reaction might be .

to focus primarily on how to salvage your career. However, just looking to rebound professionally can create a blind spot preventing you from seeing what's really going on inside you that needs repair. Both can be done simultaneously; however, if you focus only on professional recovery and don't do personal recovery work, you might find any career rehabilitation you experience to be short-lived.

Peace

TRAIN A CHILD IN THE WAY HE SHOULD GO

We're living in a time when everything about what it means to be a man is changing. Men, we have to make a change now, for our own sake and the sake of the boys who will become men after us. We have the power to do this as husbands, fathers, brothers, grandfathers, uncles, mentors, and friends. It's our responsibility to impact how present and future men will handle the Dog and empower the Master. Women, we need your help in the process.

It's our responsibility to teach the next generation the secrets to becoming a new kind of man for this new world:

- Learning to love
- Dealing with and controlling lust
- Being vulnerable and open about past pain

- Building a safe space with other men
- Building strong, transparent, and respectful relationships with women
- Maintaining a safe work environment by treating everyone as equals

Women, you are appreciated and valued beyond any words I can effectively write on this page. You've had to endure dealing with the Dog yet you're still here and have somehow found it within you to love us men, who desperately need your love. I pray for your healing, wisdom, strength, and success. I hope these truths empower you to live your best life and inspire you every step of the way.

Men, if you're ready to change the legacy of the men in your family by teaching the next generation, you must start by committing to the process of getting your own Dog under control. Work toward mastering the Dog. Get it on a strong leash and behind a strong fence. Create your safe space. Get real with your past transgressions and with the woman in your life. Make that relationship good and honest and loving. As you do that, start passing along what you know, especially to young boys.

Here are three things the young boys need from us. Mothers, these tips can apply to you too as you endeavor to raise great men.

1. **Leadership.** Nothing matters more to a young man of any age than how the men around him act. If we want boys to grow up treating people with respect, we need to

show them how it's done every day. Let's be respectful, loving, considerate, and kind to everyone we come in contact with. Deal with conflict with reason and compassion, not anger. Kids see more than we realize. Your sons are watching.

2. **Knowledge.** Take the time to sit down with your son and talk to him about the Dog, the Master, the urges, sexual harassment, safe spaces, the media stereotypes— all of it. Everything we've talked about in this book is a lesson you can pass along. Teach him that while the Dog is powerful, he doesn't have to let it control his life. Teach him what it means to be a true man of honor, courage, discipline, and fidelity.

3. **Love.** Boys who grow up loved and hugged and cared for have the foundation for a successful life. It helps them grow into manhood with deep reserves of self-love, self-respect, and confidence. So love your son. Hug him, kiss him, spend time with him, and guide him.

This is how we begin to change the legacy of the Dog forever.

PEACE

In *The Hollywood Commandments*, I said that I believed the ultimate reward for following God's purpose in your career was peace. I believe the same is true for men who discipline the

Dog and become Masters. Peace is found in a home built on faithfulness. Peace means having love, a strong family bond, self-respect, and self-control.

Peace is the goal. Peace only comes when we act with self-awareness, honor, honesty, morality, and love toward all the people in our life. The Dog doesn't care about peace, but the Master thrives on it. Train the Dog and peace will be found, even if it's been elusive for a lifetime.

This is my prayer.

Peace.

ACKNOWLEDGMENTS

I am eternally grateful for all the tremendous and divine assistance I've received to help get this book to the world. I want to thank God and my Lord and Savior Jesus Christ for the opportunity to have had the experiences that provided the seed for the wisdom in this book.

I want to thank my incredible wife, Meagan, you are God's gift to me. I want to thank Beth Adams and the great team at Howard/Atria/Simon & Schuster; my unbelievable book agents Nena Madonia and Jan Miller at Dupree Miller; the incomparable Maria Shriver, thank you for your prompting, I'm eternally grateful; my amazing publicist Clare Anne Darragh of Frank PR; my friend and longtime collaborator Tim Vandehey, thanks for your help with laying the foundation for this; my incredible social media manager Jenn DePaula at Mixtus Media; my dear friend and attorney John Meigs; my dynamic team at William Morris Endeavor; my wonderful staff at Franklin Entertainment—thank you Ally, Jessica, Katelyn, Zahra, and Brittany; to the many people that participated in being interviewed for this book, I'm forever appreciative; and to my mother, family, friends, associates, and fans—as I always say, I'm grateful for your support, thank you for your love, prayers, and help! I wouldn't be where I am without any of you.

WHAT SHOULD YOU READ NEXT?

I can't thank you enough for taking the time to read my book. I pray that it has blessed you and helped you. If you enjoyed *The Truth About Men*, and if you're looking for what to read next, please allow me to suggest my other books as well. In addition, I send out weekly inspiration about life and relationships in my free newsletter. Subscribers also get a chance to hear first about my latest books, movie projects, and other exciting things that will help them remain inspired and motivated. You can sign up here: DeVonFranklin.com.